Taking Steps To Draw Closer To GOD

Milly J

MILLY J

Victorious Publishing

United States of America

Copyright © 2019 by **Milly J**

All rights reserved. No part of this book may be reproduced or transmitted in any form or by any means, electronic or mechanical, including photocopying, recording or by any information storage and retrieval system, without written permission from the publisher, except for the inclusion of brief quotations in a review.

Victorious Publishing
Web: www.VictoriousPublishing.co
Email: VP@victoriouspublishing.co

All scripture quotations, unless otherwise indicated, are taken from the New King James Version®. Copyright © 1982 by Thomas Nelson, Inc. Used by permission. All rights reserved.

Book Layout © 2017 BookDesignTemplates.com
Photos permission used
FreeImages.com/Diane Miller
FreeImages.com/Lozba Paul
FreeImages.com/Terri-Ann Hanlon
FreeImages.com/Tom Fawls
FreeImages.com/Petre Birlea
FreeImages.com/RTK
FreeImages.com/Steven Goodwill
FreeImages.com/Emmanuel Rivet
FreeImages.com/Kym McLeod

Taking Steps To Draw Closer To God/ Milly J -New Edition.
ISBN 978-0-578-43814-6

Disclaimer

I did not write this book to remove you from daily fellowship with God or bible study, church attendance or prayer. I write this book to encourage a closer walk with God and spiritual growth. I recommend that you have a bible with you for scripture references. *"Be diligent to present yourself approved to God a worker who does not need to be ashamed, rightly dividing the word of truth,"* **2 Timothy 2:15**.

Special Message

In this book version, I will use the Hebrew name for the Son of God, Yahshua or being more general, The Messiah. You may also notice I use Yahweh, Elohim, or the Most High for God. My reasoning for using the Hebrew names is that I come to understand that everyone has a "god" and the God I'm talking about may not be the God you are thinking about. Adding the Hebrew names in this book is my way of clarifying I am talking about the God of Israel. I know there are many arguments and disagreements about the proper name of God and his Son, but in this book, I will not cater to adding dissension to the church body.

However, a funny story about name translation that happened. I went to visit the Wycliffe Discovery Center and after my tour, there was a section to print out your name in different translations, so I typed in my name and printed out the results, well I didn't recognize my name anymore! I was like, what is this? If anyone called my name in these translations, I would not answer because I wouldn't have known whom they are calling. Now it doesn't mean it was not my name, it's just for the person speaking Hebrew, or Greek, my name was spelled different from the name I was custom too. I learned that, given the country, or language a name can sound different or spelled differently, but that doesn't mean the name changed. Therefore, I encourage you to not beat yourself about not using the Hebrew names that is something you will learn along your journey to draw closer to God.

However, it is important to identify what "god" is in your heart, for me it's the God of Israel, and that is the God I am talking about in this book.

MILLY J

Acknowledgments

I thank God for having the patience to work on me and with me. I like to thank all my family members, especially my mom and my sister, and friends who always supported me in all I do. Thanks to all the readers for letting me share a word with you. Thank you!

*"And let us not grow weary while doing good, for in due season we shall reap if we do not lose heart," ~ **Galatians 6:9***

Contents

Introduction 9

Seek First the Kingdom of God 13

Trusting God 44

Making A Commitment 61

Learning to Pray 73

The Greatest Commandment 91

A Period of Testing 102

Practical Steps to Draw Closer to God 110

Test Yourself 111

Q&A 113

Conclusion 125

Salvation Time 127

Introduction

I would like to share with you how I came up with each chapter's name. I know they are simple titles but at the time, it was steps I took to draw closer to God. After years of not taking my relationship with God seriously, one day I was set on being fully committed to God and wrote out the steps to do so. I wrote out each step and a scripture to follow, below is my actual written notes from my notebook.

My plan is to:

First, Seek first the kingdom of God, Matthew 6:33, "But seek first the kingdom of God and his righteousness, and all these things shall be added to you."

Second, Trust, Proverbs 3:5-6, "Trust in the Elohim with all your heart, and lean not on your own understanding; in all your ways acknowledge him, and he shall direct your paths."

Third, Make a Commitment, Psalms 37:4-5, "Delight yourself also in Elohim, and he shall give you the desire of your heart. Commit your way to Elohim, trust also in him, and he shall bring it to pass."

Fourth, Pray, Matthew 6:6, "But you, when you pray, go into your room, and when you have shut your door, pray to your Father who is in the secret place; and your Father who sees in secret will reward you openly."

Fifth, Love, Colossians 3:14, "But above all these things put on love, which is the bond of perfection."

    I added nothing more to what you see here, I needed to get focus and doing it this way helped me. I had no intentions to write any book about drawing closer to God that was the last thing on my mind. The day I wrote this book was a glorious day, I did not go to bed until sometime late after midnight, those who know me, knows it's way past my bedtime! God gave me the energy to write the book in a few hours. I wrote the book in 2010 but I did not publish the first version until 2012. Why did I wait so long? Where was my enthusiasm to share this information? I have no idea! God timing is the best, sometimes delays are good and my hesitation contributed. I published the book but still felt I could have done better, most authors know this feeling, you feel like it is never good enough. Hence, today I added additional materials to this version because I have also grown a lot in my walk with God and it was important for me not to leave out what kept my relationship with God going as I mature as a woman.

In addition, for nine years, I volunteered at a local church as a prayer counselor and one area I notice most people struggle with was dedicating their lives to God. Many return week after week, doing the same thing. In the words of Albert Einstein, *"Insanity is doing the same thing over and over again and expecting different results."* Something was not clicking for these individuals. The relationship with God was lacking the R.E.L.A.T.I.O.N.S.H.I.P., seeing that also encouraged me to write about how others can grow spiritually and draw closer to God.

This book is simple, and that is the purpose. I wanted to keep it simple, encourage you to learn, grow and stay committed. It is the push you need without the judgment, here are the steps, here is what you need to do to accomplish them, and now it is up to you to do them. This book was not written for those who want to have a religious debate about theology, or science, and it's not for the Sadducees and the Pharisees either. This book is solely for those who both had a relationship with God and lost it along the way and for those who want to know how to draw closer to him, that is it. I have no agenda, no church, group or organization for you to take part in. I am not a prophetess, evangelist, minister, or preacher; rather I am an everyday believer that drew closer to God. I learned something that be-

MILLY J

came valuable to my life and I am sharing what I learned and hope it will work for you too. Let's get started.

TAKING STEPS TO DRAW CLOSER TO GOD

• CHAPTER 1 •

Seek First the Kingdom of God

"But seek first the kingdom of God and his righteousness, and all these things shall be added to you."

~ Matthew 6:33

In today's world in which we live in nothing is stable and nothing is promised. Unfortunately, this has included marriages, friendships, and partnerships. However, God has promised to remain the same, yesterday, today and forever, *Hebrews 13:8.* Can you trust that? Can you trust that God will show you his un-failing, unconditional love you are seeking, rather than trusting in people's conditional love? The struggle is that many believe God is far from them, however, that is so far from the truth. God is with you. He sees your pain and suffering, and He wants to make everything better for you by guiding you, but you have to let him in. A relationship is two-way street and a relationship with God does not differ from one with a physical person.

When I first accepted Yahshua as my Savior, I did not understand the concept of drawing closer to God. I thought if I prayed that I was close to him; if I went to church, then I was close to him but he showed me it was more to him, then just praying and going to church. In fact, my first year, being "born-again" I backslidden and went back to my old ways. I started to not go to church as often as I used too. I went back to watching television for hours, instead of reading my bible. I did not pray as much and I was developing a nonchalant attitude concerning the things of God. That was not his will for my life, and I am sure the Holy Spirit prompted me, but I could not hear over the sound of the television. I was stuck on doing the "basic things," going to church when I feel like it, reading my bible when I feel like it, pray a little here and there. I knew something was off but I was "too busy" watching television or doing my own things to acknowledge it. I needed to develop a relationship with God to draw closer to him, and I had to take action. Many of us are stuck at the basic and let me tell you; you do not grow or learn anything about God when you stuck with the basic. You will be like Sister Johnson, in church for twenty years with the same bad attitude or like Uncle Jimmy still cussing and getting into fights. Draw closer to God to grow from eating baby food to cutting steaks, *1 Corinthians 3:2; 1 Peter 2:2*.

Many have been told once you accepted Yahshua as your Savior-that is all you have to do. However, we have a lot more to do. God created the entire earth and planned for the stars to show up at night and the sun to be present at daytime; that is not basic. **God does extraordinary things and our relationship with him should be just as extraordinary.** I had to learn that slowly. I felt in my heart something could be more between God and I, so I took my relationship with him more seriously and I sought him.

WHAT ARE YOU SEARCHING? We often spend our time searching and seeking. We search for relationships; we search for better careers, better cars and better this and that. We spend a good amount of time glued to our phones or computers searching the internet, seeking stuff. However, *Matthew 6:33*, instructs us to seek *first* the kingdom of God and his righteousness. This scripture shows where our priorities should be, with God first. However, we have successfully distracted ourselves away from seeking God because of the direction this world has been going, **Mark 4:19**. It is natural we could conform to our environment, everyone is online, have social media accounts, we pay our bills online, shop online. However, many of us waste time, energy and money searching and seeking for things. Don't you hate it when you spent hours on the internet and still couldn't find what you were looking for? I know someone who literally spends a good amount of the day on social media accounts. I don't think they even go to sleep and it's not work related, it's not for business, this person is just nosey! God did not put you on earth to monitor other people's lives. If you have been browsing and following people lives on social media, it's time to get off online and start seeking God.

    We have to be more mindful how we are using our time. Look at your day now; did you accomplish anything fruitful that day? Remember what you sow you will reap. *If you have no seeds on the ground and you're busy watching someone online accomplish their goals and you have done nothing with your life, it's time to wake up from the "spirit of the internet."* Maybe it's your "guilty pleasure," but be warned that is a tool being used against you by Satan to keep you distracted. Aren't you tired of wasting time? I would like you to calculate the amount of hours you spend on your phone and/or on your computer doing whatever. I downloaded an app on my phone to monitor the hours I spent online and one day I spent 6 hours just browsing shopping sites, I could not believe I wasted 6 hours! Literally doing nothing, I did not even buy anything! Now **Matthew 6:33** made sense. I felt bad I would waste a good amount of my day like that. I had to learn to replace these hours of my life with something more productive, and start seeking God.

Whether its wealth, fame, relationships or material possessions, ***the time, and energy we spend looking for mundane things, we could be doing something more productive.*** Your time is precious here on earth and many of us only realize this as we get older. You begin to realize life was not about seeking opportunities after opportunities, watching what others are doing with their lives, and looking for this and that, but it is about seeking God, being surrounded by your love ones, having positive friendships and relationships and enjoying life as God intended. None of these things can be purchase and that is what makes them special. God would prefer us to use our time and energy to search and seek him. He promises in his word that everything we need, everything we desire, whatever you are looking for, he will provide but our focus should be on him. It is as if he knew we were going to be side tracked and he gave us the heads up in **Matthew 6:33**.

Many of our searching and seeking other things comes from what we desire, mostly worldly gains. We do not want to miss out on what everyone else is doing or have, so we search and search. God doesn't want us to worry and be fretful in life although you will experience worry and anxiety but by no means is this his desire for your life. His desire is for us to seek him and rely on him and not on ourselves or the issues of life. *"Therefore I say to you, do not worry about your life, what you will eat, or what you will drink; nor about your body, what you will put on. Is not life more than food and the body more than clothing? Look at the birds of the air, for they neither sow nor reap nor gather into barns; yet your Heavenly Father feeds them. Are you not of more value than they? Which of you by worrying can add one cubit to his stature? "So why do you worry about clothing? Consider the lilies of the field, how they grow; they neither toil nor spin; and yet I say to you that even Solomon in all his glory was not arrayed like one of these. Now if God so clothes the grass of the field which today is, and tomorrow is thrown into the oven, will he not much more clothe you, O you of little faith? "Therefore, do not worry, saying, "What shall we eat? Or what shall we drink? Or what shall we wear? For after all these things the Gentiles seek. For your Heavenly Father knows you need all these things," Matthew 6:25-32.* God got this, so tell worry to go away and fear to go back out the door it came from, enough wasting your time on mundane searching, you do not have time for that! Your time is for seeking the Most High. I will let you in on a little secret; this world will always be filled with problems until God says otherwise, and it will not be changing soon, so while you here on earth focus instead on what matters.

WHAT IS IN YOUR HEART? The most important thing to realize about seeking God is that you do not have to leave the country and live in a cave to find him and draw closer to him.

TAKING STEPS TO DRAW CLOSER TO GOD

You do not have to stop life and become a priest or nun. All you have to do is have a desire in your heart to seek him and he will fulfill that desire. *"May he grant you according to your heart's desire, and fulfill all your purpose," Psalm 20:4.* Seeking God starts with your heart. *The word seeking involves locating and discovering something.* To locate and discover something, you have to set your mind to finding what you are looking for. Before you can set your mind, something in your heart had to move you to want to search and locate whatever you desire. If you do not have a desire to seek God, you will not take the time to draw closer to him. It's like in a relationship, if a person does not have a desire in their heart to seek after you, then they will not waste their time trying to pursue you or to draw closer to you. What is in your heart about God will eventually show in your actions. *"Keep your heart with all diligence, for out of it spring the issues of life," Proverbs 4:23.*

When I finally decided to truly seek God with all my heart, mind, and soul, I had reached a point in my life where I could not see myself without him. There were so much things going on in the world I didn't want to be part of and I wanted to hide under God's wings. God was my only protection. I kept feeling a tug to seek him and really get to know him more than ever before. Saying I now followed Yahshua was not enough. I was not satisfied with just going to church and listening to sermons anymore. He wanted more from me, and I wanted to know more about him spiritually. The desire to seek him was strong and so intense that all my conversations were about him. I didn't know how to have a conversation with others without bringing him up. Many did not understand my desire. However, that desire helped me draw closer to him. I wouldn't give up my desire to seek him because of how others thought of me. It is like when you first accepted Yahshua as your Savior, you are so excited and you wanted to tell everyone the good news. As I got older, I learned to balance everything and learned not everyone will be receptive.

You will run into people who will say you are "too spiritual" because they don't understand your relationship with the Most High or haven't comprehend him. When you are in the presence of spiritual people, you will know it because you will feel the presence of God around them. You will have a sense that there is something "different" about this person or may desire to be around them more often. If you encounter people telling you that, you are "too spiritual" respond with a thank you. This means you are going in the right direction. There is nothing wrong with being spiritually connected to God and allowing his word to take effect in your life. Many people get turn off when you start to "change" for the better. Some people like the old you, that cuss, party, drink, committing fornication. As you draw closer to God and let these things go, and apply the bible to your life, many will draw away from you because they feel like they can't "fit" in anymore. For many, instead of finding out what are you doing to get better they run away in fear they can't get better.

TAKING STEPS TO DRAW CLOSER TO GOD

To draw closer to the God, your desire needs to be intense, unchangeable, and consistent no matter the circumstance. God has to be first and he will constantly put you through test and trials to show you he will come first. For instance, there are times I get upset about something not going my way and I want to take it out on God. I would literally think this in my head, "Why didn't God let me have it?" "Does he really care about me?" "This is so unfair!" I kid you not, it was just a thought, I haven't even spoken it aloud, then God spoke to my heart by allowing someone else to speak something encouraging about the thing I was mad about God with and it literally humbled me! That made me realize that, one, God is watching and know our hearts and inner thoughts, and two, I was being selfish and not putting him first, three, I had to get focus and ask God, what is it you want me to do?, *Proverbs 3:5-6*. I learned it was not about me, my selfishness, or my lack of understanding, but it was about allowing God to be first and guiding me through this life.

Learn to examine your heart every day. You will find God will speak directly to what is in your heart about him, your situations, and what is going on in this world. As you begin your search and seek God, ask yourself these questions; how strong is my desire to seek God? Am I seeking him with all my heart, mind and soul? *"So he answered and said, you shall love God your Elohim with all your heart, with all your soul, with all your strength, and with all your mind, and your neighbor as yourself," Luke 10:27*. Your heart, mind and soul have to work together so you can successfully draw closer to God. If your heart is not in it, your mind will not think about it, and your soul will just be waiting on you to decide on what you want to do. We have to be mindful that we are not approaching the Most High with just lip service, *Matthew 15:8 says, "These people draw near to me with their mouth, and honor me with their lips, but their heart is far from me…"* Remember teamwork make the dream work!

Why are you seeking God in the first place? What do you desire from him? What kind of relationship do you want to establish with him? *Seeking God involves taking action and all the action is on your part.* The amount of action you take will be based on how strong the desire in your heart is to draw closer to him. If you are wondering, can I develop this desire? Yes, you can. The desire to seek God comes from what you have heard about him. What you think about him, what you know about him, it comes from your life experiences and other people's life experiences and it comes from him calling you, *"God is faithful, by whom you were called into the fellowship of his Son, Yahshua,"* 1 *Corinthians 1:9.*

After you become "born-again" meaning you have accepted to get into a relationship with God and acknowledge his Son Yahshua died for our sins, and was risen and now can be call one of his children, the Holy Spirit comes to live in you (in your spirit), *"but the Helper, the Holy Spirit, whom the Father will send in my name, he will teach you all things, and bring to your remembrance all things that I said to you,"* John 14:26. The

Holy Spirit is a gift from the Most High to be our guide on earth. The Holy Spirit is that inner voice telling you what to do and helps direct your steps. Keep in mind, you have to learn to listen, and not with your physical ears, but with your heart. *Your heart is your spiritual ears.*

When you are developing a desire to seek after God, the Holy Spirit will prompt you to do this or do that. For instance, the Holy Spirit may show you what scripture you need for an issue that may be going on in your life. He may direct you to a certain book, person or church to help you with your desire to draw closer to him. He is your Helper and as a child of God, he already supplied all of your needs. *He knows the direction you need to go, so trust your inner spirit directing you.* As you draw closer to God, he will also draw closer to you. *"Draw near to God and he will draw near to you. Cleanse your hands, you sinners; and purify your hearts, you double-minded," James 4:8.* I encourage you to yield to God.

IS GOD A PRIORITY? Drawing closer to God will require you to seek *his will* and making *his will* the priority in your life above everything else. ***Prioritize will be the key to being able to seek him and staying on track.*** As you prioritize your life to search and seek him, you are enabling yourself to draw closer to him. I can tell you from my personal experiences, when I placed other things, such as school, work, relationships and hobbies before the Most High, times where I should have experienced joy, I experienced frustration instead, because my priorities were out of order. I always felted nervous, tired, overwhelmed, unfulfilled and anxious, all because I made these other things first and more important in my life instead of seeking God first. Although from the outside looking in, my life may have "seem in order" by the world standard. I was in school, I work, I have hobbies, I attended church, but spiritually I was out of order.

I could not draw closer to him with everything else being first. After making God my priority, life was less stressful and more peaceful. I stop depending on myself to make it through the day, but instead depending on God strength to go through the day, *Isaiah 41:10*. You will see how the Most High will make a way out of difficult roads on your journey to draw closer to him. You will learn how to react more positive rather than how the world expect you to react during difficult times. Your problems will not disappear automatically but you will learn how to deal with them when they appear and God will show you how.

Seeking God will also be a continuous process. Make your mind up you will seek him for the rest of your life, *"If then you were raised with Yahshua, seek those things which are above, where Yahshua is, sitting at the right hand of God. Set your mind on things above, not on things on the earth," Colossians 3:1-2.* Your relationship with God is like a relationship with a person if you stop working on the relationship, eventually it will not work out and fade out. *If you want to build your relationship with God, put in the effort to see it through all the days of your life.* I know for some hearing the words "putting in the effort" can be overwhelming, but do not be dismay! God will bless you exceedingly, when you make him first, *"For You, O Elohim, will bless the righteousness; with favor, you will surround him as with a shield," Psalm 5:12.*

Seeking God daily will ensure his constant presence in your life and situations. The best thing you can do, is start your day with God and end it with him, *"My voice shalt thou hear in the morning, O Elohim; in the morning will I direct my prayer unto thee, and will look up," Psalm 5:3*. You cannot stop seeking him because you got a "revelation" on how to seek him, you have to continually be searching and discovering whom he is; seeking his character, his truth, which is his word (the bible). **Seeking him should be a lifestyle, it is what you do and not just something you talk about.**

WHAT WILL YOU LET GO? As you seek him, you also have to let go of everything that is tormenting you or keeping you from seeking him. Clear your mind of distractions. Let go of all the thoughts that say you cannot draw closer to God, whether these thoughts are from guilt, shame, pride, fear, doubt, or what you did last night, last year, ten years ago, *"There is therefore now no condemnation to those who are in Yahshua, who do not walk according to the flesh, but according to the Spirit," Romans 8:1*. If you will take notice, having thoughts of guilt, shame, fear, are all emotions base on the flesh. What you are "feeling" at the moment, it is not based on the Spirit. The Spirit has self-control, *Galatians 5:22-25*. If you are walking according to the Spirit, no one may condemn you because you are making it right with God. God wants you to walk in the Spirit, his Spirit, not by your flesh. You are now the righteousness of God so take hold of that and embrace his grace. Here is a little side note on grace: *grace is not an excuse to continue in sin*. It is not an excuse to remain in your guilt, shame or fear but to realize that grace allows us not to remain in these things. The spiritual definition of grace is "unmerited favor" of God. It means that God is doing something for us we cannot do in our own effort, something we do not even deserve, *"For by grace you have been saved through faith, and that not of yourselves; it is the gift of God, not of works, lest anyone should boast," Ephesians 2:8-9.*

Here is another "to do" to add to your list when seeking God, you will also have to keep your distant from people who are distracting your walk with him. Remove yourself from hanging around negative people, people who are against the word of God and worldly; those individuals that have one foot in the church and the other foot in the world or both foot in the world, *"Do not be deceived: evil company corrupts good habit," 1 Corinthians 15:33.* Personally for me I don't want to pick up other people's bad habits. I don't want to pick up the habit of drinking, gossiping, hating, being negative about life, I can live without these things!

When I say having "one or two foot in the world", I am talking about those who know the truth, are in the truth, understand what the bible say and still do the complete opposite of what God says. They deliberately ignore what God says to do, and do what is pleasing to them and it's not coming from a lack of understanding. I am not referring to people, who do not know God, or have not truly comprehended him or the bible, or just struggling in their walk with God. You will need to be around people who support your new life walk and encourage your walk with God. You need to be around those who truly believe the word and are doers of the word and not just hearers, *"But be doers of the word, and not hearers only, deceiving yourselves. For if anyone is a hearer of the word and not a doer, he is like a man observing his natural face in a mirror; for he observes himself, goes away, and immediately forgets what kind of man he was. But he who looks into the perfect law of liberty and continues in it, and is not a forgetful hearer but a doer of the work, this one will be blessed in what he does," James 1:22-25.*

Now do not go around putting others down just because you are drawing closer to God. Do not be that person holding up a stop sign- saying they cannot talk to you or be around you because they are not "believers like you" or have not reached "your level" of spirituality. **The more spiritual you get, the more humble you should be.** Everyone one has their own walk in life, some choose to walk it with the Most High, some struggle on their way there, and some choose not to, but that does not mean they are not human just as you are. ***Always remain humble, remain open to teaching others who want to learn what you are learning yourself.*** The people I'm referring to about distancing yourself from are those who blatantly try to distract you from drawing closer to God knowing your desire to do so; or mocking God, and many do it without realizing it when they live a double life; or mocking you because you are a believer, or those who think it's okay to sin "a little" today and ask for forgiveness tomorrow, not realizing sin still has consequences and want you to take part in sin with them, those are the folks I am talking about. Those who continuously show you through their actions they do not care to change and want to keep you down, remember misery loves company. You must pray for the spirit of discernment so you can quickly identify those who truly want to understand and help you walk your journey with God from those who are just trying to pull your leg and pull you away from him.

In the book of Genesis, God had asked Abraham to leave his country, and leave his relatives before he can bless him. God knew if Abraham had the wrong people surrounding him that Abraham might not have obeyed him. Abraham may have not been able to hear his voice either, *Genesis 12:1-4*. If you do not change your surroundings, you are prone to going back to your old ways and draw away from the Most High. It will not be easy, but it is necessary. **This does not mean you withdraw your love from them, it may mean you have to distance yourself for a little while or you have to set boundaries.** When you know better, you can do better and you can help others do the same. The blind leading the blind just does not work.

I recall hearing a story about a man who wanted to stop using drugs; in fact, he was in rehab but guess who was still using drugs? His best friend! Therefore, you see sometimes the people closest to you can harm you. When you are trying to draw closer to God, be very mindful, mindful of your surroundings, mindful of your friends, co-worker and yes even your family members. No one is exempt! Get accountability partners, people who can help you stay committed and focus. Someone who can be a teacher, a helper and a true friend who want to see you grow spiritually.

Adjust your schedule, examine how you spend your time, and pay attention to the things you look at, read, and listen to. You will have to be careful about even the places you hang out at, and whom you are hanging with. When you do not know whether what you are doing or watching is right, ask yourself, what would the Most High want me to be doing? Would Yahshua be hanging at the club with Paul, James and Matthew *(His disciples)*? Would the Most High be sitting around smoking with the Angels? You know the right thing to do, and if you don't, let the Holy Spirit guide you, it's his job! That feeling that is telling you do not go to that club, listen to it! That hutch telling you do not date that person, listen to it! That voice telling you do not touch that cake, listen to it! That is the Holy Spirit at work.

God wants to bless you. He promises to bless those who seek after him, *Psalm 34:10, Psalm 1:1-3; Psalm 119:2; Hebrews 11:6; Lamentations 3:25*, so not only will you draw closer to him, but you come out blessed! He promises to provide us with what we desire when we seek him. I would like to clarify this "desire" **it will be within the limits of what he considers a blessing to you.** I know many churches are preaching what some are calling, the "prosperity gospel" but guess what? There is no such gospel and not everyone on earth will be millionaires and billionaires, not everyone will live in a mansion. In fact, not everyone like big homes, some people are content with a regular house or even a tiny home, as you may have seen from the tiny house movement. Are you only seeking God so he can bless you? **Learn to be content with what he has blessed you with now. If it is your destiny to have more, he will give you more. There is nothing too big for God to do, but he will always do it within what he thinks is best for you. Sometimes we get so busy seeking other things we forget to seek the spiritual things first.**

Amid our busyness seeking other things, we lose our peace to all the things that were never meant to be first place in our lives. When we give other things and people priority over the Most High, we are also out of the will of God for our lives. Stop letting things, such as careers, money, hobbies, material possessions, relationships, the internet, social media, have more control over you than seeking God. Seeking other things before seeking God limits your time to develop a relationship with him. If you are busy doing other things, examine where the Most High fit in your schedule. He was meant to be first and seeking him is the first step to drawing closer to him.

WHAT DOES GOD WANT FROM ME? To seek him you have to know how he thinks, how he wants you to live, what is his will for your life and all the answers for these questions are in the bible. God gives us instructions and guidance in the bible. In your journey to draw closer to him, you will see this for yourself. *God reveals himself through his word.* Because of this, it will be imperative you study your bible. The bible will be the most important book in your life, read it, study it, use it and live by it!

WHAT ABOUT CHURCH? Although some may feel church attendance is unnecessary to draw closer to God, finding a group of believers, will be necessary in your life at some point. Trust me; I know personally the church struggle, especially these days it has been a journey and a struggle in finding the right church, one that is teaching the word correctly or even following it. However, there are certain things you will not understand about the bible without additional help. That is why God assigned preachers, bishops, elders, and teachers on earth, *1 Peter 5:1-4;2 Timothy 3:16-17; Mark 16:15; Matthew 28:18-20; Titus 1:5-9.* When you attend a bible based church or meeting with a group of like-minded individuals, you "should" receive further understanding and revelation. I had to quote "should" because that is an expectation but that does not mean it will happen all the time, especially if you are in the wrong church or group. I know some of you can come up with many reasons church attendance is unnecessary and you do not want any part of it and I will not disagree with you! Like I said, I know the struggle!

When I moved and was looking for a church, all I can say is, oh my goodness! I could not believe the teachings people are sitting under! I mean some churches I could not tell you if I was attending church, a concert, a play or conference. Church is not the same today. Some churches today seem to be more interested in providing entertainment rather than helping you grow spiritually. Many are filled with programs, plays, and conferences to keep you entertain and "busy" that they do not have the time for revivals, prayer meetings, fasting, and spiritual things. There are some churches that still do these things but it's very rare to find nowadays. I have sat in a church for years, where I didn't agree with everything the church did, how some people were being treated, or how scriptures were being used. I was still a "babe" in the church so there was a lot I had to learn spiritually. I had to take the time to seek God myself. I didn't rely only on the church for teachings but the church helped me get started. As I study the bible more, it lead me to see that something is not right here. However, I will not take away what I learned from that church and it helped me in some aspect. My season for being in that church was over and God allowed me to move on. I can recall the day I knew it was over. I had moved to another state, went back to my hometown, and visited the church and I could feel a spiritual disconnect with that church, and I knew from there not to go back, it was over.

    I kept looking for other churches in the state I live in, but nothing seems right. I went to God about this and he reminded me of something so simple, "is he limited to just being in the church?" "Is that the only place I can find him?" And the answer is no, God is everywhere and his spirit lives in me. Many pastors will preach to you that you shouldn't leave the church if you haven't found a replacement or that leaving "their" church will disconnect you from receiving your blessings. Beware of these kinds of teachings, especially where someone wants to "control" your decisions. Many pastors and leaders are narcissistic and will try to control their members with threats, or having others members shunning those who leave, or making contemptuous comments about their past members. When I see and hear these things it shows me their true colors, and that they are not serving God or the people but want the people to serve them and their desires. The fact a man, whether pastor, a bishop or an elder thinks they are better teachers than God is preposterous. They are to be servants of God not God himself.

God allowed me not to be worried about finding a church instead for three years I studied under God only. While allowing God to be my Teacher, God showed me how many churches left him completely out of the church and that, many are running their own corporation calling it a church. He showed me many churches are completely man made, and that everything was catered to emotionally and financially move people to the church but not to draw them closer to him. He showed me that many leaders have fallen into a snare because of their own heart desires and because they refused to repent, their darkness will come to surface in the light. He begins to revealed things I was blind too. Many times we on the go and we never question certain behaviors. In fact, some leaders teach that you shouldn't "question" them because they are "anointed." However, you may question anything that affects your relationship with God. A true leader doesn't instill fear unto others, but rather is humbled to teach. God also revealed that many "believers" stayed in the dark because of tradition, and that they felt more comfortable following the masses rather than being face with being challenged by opposition because of their beliefs. When I was in the church, I was oblivious to these things because you are taught that church is the "good" place, it's "safe", it's where God is, it's where you will find the "truth", no "devil" can come there, and everyone is "kind" but God was saying the opposite. Now this is my personal experience, and it doesn't apply to every church, but that is what God revealed and it may not be something he has revealed to you or reveal to you yet.

Another thing, God called me out of was the celebration of many manufactured holidays. Most major holidays some churches celebrate is nowhere in the bible, yet many churches take part in them religiously. I did my research in the bible and I could find none of it in there. After he reveals this, I stop taking part, some holidays I didn't care for anyway and didn't celebrate, but some I did not think of the spiritual impact it was having on me. For me, the spiritual impact was where was God in all of it? He was nowhere in it, it was completely man made based on someone else imagination. How could I continue to celebrate something that others are saying God is in it when I clearly see he is not? Why is that we continuously take manufactured ideas and try to pass them as God ideas? God doesn't need help! Many will say it's okay to do these things because they have added God in it, but ponder on this, why does God have to be added? Now many will argue that we are under "grace" and that is "Old Testament thinking" and we are living in the "New Testament" but these same people are still taking scriptures and preaching out of the Old Testament, pay attention. If they are living in the "New Testament" then nowhere, should they be using the "Old Testament" but those with spiritual understanding will know the entire bible both, old and new is relevant today as it was 3000 years ago. This was my personal experience. Whether you celebrate, take part in these holidays and traditions are entirely up to you and what God has revealed to you specifically.

Now that God has given me a better understanding and taught me how to discern, I know exactly what to look for when looking for a church. However, he also showed me that going to church would not make me more "spiritual." It's more about me taking the time to develop a relationship with him, whether in or outside of the church. Attending church was one way to draw closer to him but I was not limited to just going to church to seek him. Therefore, I understand the hesitation many have with churches today. The church is not perfect, but there are some good churches out there. Maybe you are still hurt from what others have done or said about you in the church and don't want to go through that again; maybe you are tired of giving to the building fund and twenty years has passed and there is no building in sight. Whatever your reasons, I want to encourage you to keep in mind you are seeking and searching after the Most High, he should be your priority and focus. No

TAKING STEPS TO DRAW CLOSER TO GOD

one is perfect; therefore, you cannot expect to find a church with perfect people, perfect pastors, and perfect leaders. There will be a time when all saints of the church will be called to perfection. In the meantime, pray for God to reveal his will for the church to the people at the church. Bring it to God attention through prayer, let him handle it and focus on seeking, and searching God with all your heart, mind and soul, especially if you believe God called you to a specific church or group.

If you desire to draw closer to the God, you will need to find some form of teaching, meaning finding someone or a group of people who are rightly dividing the word, who knows the truth, who are drawing you closer to the God and not away with vain teachings, *Hebrews 10:24-25. Remember the church is not a building but the people.* You do not have to go looking for a "church building," you need to find like-minded people, and God focused. Be just as careful with "groups" as you do with churches. Many have been led astray by cult leaders. Everyone who screams "God" may not be talking about your God. Some have created their own god or made themselves a god. If you want to attend a church but are struggling with the decision to go, I will suggest you spend time in prayer and ask God to lead you to a church or a group. As you wait for direction from the Most High, you can also view video teachings from that church you want to attend. Listen to pastor (s) preaching, take notes; are they rightly dividing the word? Is the teaching based on the spiritual growth or worldly gains? Write out questions you come up with and do the research!

Do not get caught up in following churches and pastors because of popularity, fame, and wealth or whom they are connected to, but take heed at whom you are following and what you are being taught. You will be surprise how many scriptures are being misused by people in ministry. I have seen scriptures twisted to fit the sermons and get people to "move" in the direction that church want people to go or what they wanted the people to do or purchase, and it was not even biblically. I heard sermons being taught just to get the church to give more not to help the homeless, or the oppress, *Proverbs 14:31; Proverbs 21:13; Proverbs 19:17; 1 Timothy 5:8; Isaiah 1:17; Deuteronomy 15:7-8; James 1:27*, but for themselves and "their church vision." Be careful under which teachings you allow yourself and family to sit under. **When your focus is on following "the man," you will fall prey to being manipulated, deceived, and side-tracked. No one can guarantee you entry to Heaven.** If you want to draw closer to the God be proactive and look for resources to help you achieve your goal.

When I sought God and his ways of doing things, the benefits were life changing. It was not entirely easy and a smooth road. The closer you draw to God the more he will reveal to you spiritually. At times, you will find you cannot trust many people. **He will also expose you, your thoughts, and what is deep down in your heart**. It will not be all fun and games, in fact, all hell may break loose. However, for every challenge you face, he will make you wiser and stronger. For instance, when difficult situations arise, before I would cry and pout about them, now if difficult situations arise, I can keep my emotions in control and seek the Most High for wisdom concerning my situation instead of crying about them and he always worked it out. I got my peace back making God first. I can go to God and the bible and get solutions for my problems. I am also no longer concern with what is happening around me, I stay focus on my relationship with God and know all will be well. If you stay up watching the news or the latest world events, you will live in fear for the rest of your life. Get your mind off this world and focus on the Most High, the day will take care of itself. Once you understand that the Most High is guiding you and protecting you, you will not spend your time fussing about what is going around in this world or even in your life, but you'll know God has your back. This world wants us to live in fear but God wants us to live in peace, **2 Timothy 1:7**, so choose one.

God is so good he gave us the heads up and instructs us to, *"Seek first the kingdom of God..."* He will give you the wisdom, the understanding, and he knows you cannot do it alone. You will need him. You will need to lean on him and put him first so he can guide you through life. If you have a thirst to draw closer to the God, take action and seek him now. Your ability to seek God will require you to eliminate all that keep you from seeking him. He wants to see you grow spiritually and not just materially. The same way you desire a relationship with him, he desires one with you. Don't delay, *Isaiah 55,* as you seek God first, trust.

Seek First the Kingdom Of God

Chapter Key Points

- Seeking God starts with a desire in your heart, then your mind will be set to finding him.

- Be doers of the word not just a hearer.

- Learn to prioritize. God must be first.

- Change your surroundings.

Seek First the Kingdom Of God

"Seek God and his strength; seek his face evermore!"
~ 1 Chronicles 16:11

Checklist

- Eliminate the things and people that keep you from seeking the Most High* *(Sin, pride and fear are things that will keep you from seeking God)*.
- Tackle priorities- Place God first on the list.
- Create a bible reading/studying plan.
- Make a prayer list.
- Develop a daily schedule to spend time and fellowship with God through bible reading, studying, prayer, church/group attendance or fellowship.

Notepad

_____
_____
_____
_____
_____
_____
_____
_____
_____

MILLY J

Seek First the Kingdom Of God

Scriptures to Meditate

~Deuteronomy 4:29
"But from there you will seek God, and you will find him if you seek him with all your heart and with all your soul."

~Psalm 9:10

"And those who know your name will put their trust in you; for you, Elohim, have not forsaken those who seek you."

~Psalm 63:1

"O God, you are my Elohim; early will I seek you; my soul thirsts for you; my flesh longs for you in a dry and thirsty land where there is no water."

~Proverbs 8:17

"I love those who love me and those who seek me diligently will find me."

~Jeremiah 29:13

"And you will seek me and find me, when you search for me with all your heart."

TAKING STEPS TO DRAW CLOSER TO GOD

Seek First the Kingdom Of God

Prayer

 My Elohim, I want to know and do your will. I purpose in my life to seek you and your kingdom first at all times. You are my priority Yahweh. I love you with all my heart, mind and soul. I desire to draw closer to you. Help me seek your ways and seek your face daily. I pray that you will direct my steps, so I can draw closer to you and may seek you first all the days of my life.

MILLY J

• CHAPTER 2 •

Trusting God

"Trust in God with all your heart, and lean not on your own understanding; in all your ways acknowledge him, and he shall direct your paths."

~ Proverbs 3:5-6

WHOM CAN I TRUST? Have you been in a relationship where you did not trust a spouse, co-worker, friend, or family member? Trusting is a major issue in relationships, without it there is no point of moving on. To trust or not to trust is a question we face almost every day in our lives. These days people make it difficult to trust anyone or anything. Every time you turn around for a second, someone is scheming a plan to kill, steal, or destroy you, **John 10:10**. I think the reason many of us either trust so little or trust too much, is because we forget what trusting really means. *Trusting involves depending on, hoping in and confiding in.* Many people will prove to you they are not trustworthy through their actions and often we ignore the "signs." Many do things to others and think nothing of it but it speaks volumes on your ability to trust them again. Many friendships have been broken because someone felt they could break the trust and share another friend's personal information with others. Sometimes, it's not a friendship that is broken but a relationship because of a cheating or a lying spouse. On the other end, many have been killed, robbed, deceived, because they trusted someone too much. Many fall prey to "friendly faces," "smiley faces," charismatic individuals and people can "appear" genuine but they are really wolves in sheep's clothing, two faced, **Matthew 7:15**. We all go through something with someone that has taught us how to trust.

However, regardless of what and who caused you to have "trust issues," trusting will be a necessary ingredient if you are going to draw closer to God. Trusting involves knowing someone's character and ability. *Someone who is trustworthy is someone you can trust in what he or she says and his or her ability to do what he or she say. Trusting is having the confidence in what they say.* Anyone can say they trust someone. However, if that trust is with limitations or doubts, that is an indication you really do not trust them. Trusting is a firm belief deep inside you that no matter what happen you can depend on that person. God requires the same trust, with no limitations or doubts. *There is no doubt in trust. If doubt enters, trust is not there.*

HOW DO I TRUST GOD? To trust God is to believe with no doubts he will do what he said he would do. Trusting him is not based on how you are feeling like the trust we have for each other. When you trust God, you trust him no matter what the outcome. It has to be unconditional. Even if your prayers are not answered or not answered as you would like them to be, trust him. *This is where faith works miracles in our lives.* Faith is described in *Hebrews 11:1, "Now faith is the substance of things hoped for, the evidence of things not seen."* This entails that you have trust in what God said he will do and faith helps you execute that trust. For instance, let us say you are trusting him to bring you out of a bad situation; your faith helps you stay in that trust you have in God. Since you haven't seen him do anything to get you out of that situation, yet because you trust him to do what he says, he will do, you believe. *Trust, faith and belief all work together.* The trust you have in the God must be stable, constant, resistant, and permanent and fixed in place. That trust cannot be moved by other people's fear, your own fears, bad situations, outside circumstances, political movements, or even bill collectors.

You must decide to trust him. God will not force you to trust him. You make that decision by your own free will. Second, you must surrender to him. ***Surrendering to God means to give up and let him have complete control over your life and decisions.*** This may sound weird to some and might be difficult for others to do, but you will make that decision, eventually. Although, God has given us free will, it is not so we can think we can do it all on our own. The quicker you surrender to the trusting process the more smoothly it will go. ***If you want to fight, God will be your perfect match.*** God will allow you to be tested in that thing you don't want to give up or let go. You have to be able to trust him with your life, your goals, dreams, and family, with everything. Trust him even when bad things are happening to you, your children and around you.

Remember, all the things God said he would do, happened. Throughout the entire bible you will find people who have placed their trust in the Most High and everything he promises to do for them, he did it. He promised to bring the children of Israel out of Egypt, and he did it, *Exodus 20:2*. He promised Sarah (Sarai) that she will have a baby out of her own womb, and he did it, *Genesis 17:17-19; Genesis 18:13-14; Genesis 21:2-3*, and she were in her nineties! As you read your bible, repeatedly, you will find those who lay down their plans and trusted the Most High to bring them out of situations, he did it.

Examine your own life, I am sure you can find situations where you thought there was no way out, but you trusted in God for a way out, and he did it. It might not have been on "your" timetable or how "you" would like it to be, but God got it done.

    Keep in mind, trusting God is not about getting what you want from him, but it is about building a relationship. Third, get rid of the "I want" and "I need" mentality. Get rid of the "I." You cannot get upset with God and not trust him anymore because he did not do what "you" want him to do. That thinking is based on selfish motives. The Most High is not moved by selfishness. Trusting God brings more satisfaction than your selfishness can ever bring, **Psalm 34:8**. When you blame God, losing trust in him, mad at him, examine your motive and reasoning. Why have you lost faith and trust in God? Remember our relationship with the Most High is a process and he wants to mature us before he can bless us with certain things. I encourage you to examine your thoughts concerning trusting him.

    Selfishness will only keep you away from drawing closer to God. I know this personally, I spent a great part of my early twenties in selfishness and no good deed came out of it. God is a patient and I am thankful he protected me from many horrors because of my selfishness. Where I should have waited, I moved forward like a speeding bull only to be hit head on. Where I should have listened, I ended up with the short end of the stick. I had to pack selfishness in a luggage and put it out of my house! Selfishness will destroy you, your relationship with God and with others. I remember when I was younger before I was "saved" I wouldn't compromise with anyone about anything! I stood my ground, even when I'm losing! I was childish and lacked wisdom to deal with others. It was my way or the highway, there was no in between. It was all about me, me, me and me did not nothing for me but caused me pain!

When I looked back at my childish behaviors now, I was acting just like Pharaoh, where he wouldn't let the people go, **See Chapters Exodus 1-14**. My heart was hardened in understanding others and letting them get a "pass." Just as God harden Pharaoh's heart, *Exodus 10:1*, he allowed my heart to be hardened so I can see not how bad the other person was but how bad I was! It was a big lesson for me and to this day, I am careful to examine my heart and make sure my motives are pure and that I'm not harboring anything against anyone. When people do something bad or talk bad about me, I give it to God and let him deal with them. My heart will stay free of anything that can hinder my relationship with him and block my blessings. I learned my "heart" lesson! Heart checks are no joke! It's so freeing to let go, and let God, *1 Thessalonians 5:15; 2 Corinthians 13:11; Proverbs 10:12; Proverbs 20:22; Ephesians 4:30-32; 1 Peter 3:9*. People who had "done" me wrong, can't understand why I am so silent about it. I won't go around telling people what they have done, I don't talk about it, nor will I waste my time pondering on it. Once I give it to God, it's for God to deal with.

Some people want a reaction from you but why give them that power over your emotions? Sometimes we think our actions towards others will teach them a lesson, but I've learned the best Teacher is God, *Psalm 6:1; Romans 2:8-11; Romans 12:19; Proverbs 25:21-22; Psalms 7:8-16; 1 Corinthians 4:5; 2 Corinthians 5:10; Ecclesiastes 12:14; Matthew 12:36.* I personally wouldn't want to mess with God! Do your heart checks and get over yourself and out of selfishness! I am a much better mature woman now, thanks to God and putting down my selfishness so I can trust him to work in my life.

Don't wait for your life to be out of control to start trusting God to take control! Life already feels like a maze, why try to figure the path on your own? Let go and trust God! Take the time to examine others that put their trust in him and their results. Read about Abraham, Noah, David and others in the bible who trusted God in everything. Reading about them, will build up your faith and trust in him. You will also see they had some struggle with trust and many of us do. Abraham laughed and question God about Sarah having a baby at an old age, *Genesis 17:17.* I think we all would have laughed! That didn't change God thought about the matter. Noah had one of the biggest challenges, building a cruise size ship with no technology! However, he trusted God, *Genesis 6:22; Hebrews 11:7.* Can you imagine building a cruise size ship and being mocked in the process? I could imagine every time someone passed by Noah they were mocking and laughing at him but he trusted God through it all. Have you been in situations where people laughed at your dreams or something God said will happen in your life and they didn't believe but you remain in God's trust? Daniel had to trust God in the Lion's den, **Daniel 6**; The Hebrew boys had to trust God in the fiery furnace, **Daniel 3**. Repeatedly you will find many had to simply trust and activate their faith in the Most High to save them. Most of us if placed in these situations will probably fall apart, or die, but we now have plenty of examples on trusting God and having the faith in him to help us. How can you draw closer to the God if you do not trust him? Ponder on that. It will not work; there will always be a missing ingredient in that relationship. If you cannot trust God, you cannot draw closer to him either.

HOW DO I LET GOD TAKE CONTROL? Identify areas where you are struggling to trust God. I already had "issues" with trusting others and being from New York didn't make it easier! I was taught from a very early age to not trust anyone, but the Most High is different. He does not have an agenda or motives against you. He will not go around talking bad about you. He will not put your personal business out there for everyone's ears. He is the best person to confide in. Trusting God will help you learn how to trust others. My favorite part is that God already warned us not to put our trust in humankind, *Psalm 146:3; Psalm 118:8-9; Micah 7:5; Jeremiah 17:5; Isaiah 31:1*. He knew there would be people that will break your trust in them and many relationships have been almost irreparable. However, I wouldn't be surprise these people didn't ask and prayed to God whether they should be in these friendships or relationships, and most of us don't. Many friendships are ruined because someone trusted the wrong person in their circle. As much as many think, they can be "friends" with everyone that is so far from the truth. Some people are troublemakers, gossipers, liars that will spread false information about you and will destroy you or your friendships with others. Trust and pray that God will place the right people in your surroundings and life that you can trust, but he needs to be part of your life in order for him to do that.

Stop thinking "you" know people. The only time I knew someone was when the Holy Spirit revealed the person's true intentions. I couldn't see their wicked intentions against me on the surface. You need to be discerning when dealing with people. Some people put on a real effort to be fake and conceal their evilness. I'm always mindful of people who tell me "trouble follows them" or "it's always everyone else fault when the relationship did not work out" or my favorite one, "no one likes them." These statements raise my eyebrows and I pay close attention. This is not just for friendships, you should also be mindful of the relationships you are getting into with a man or a woman. I recall a man I was interested in working in the same building I was, and we had a few quick elevator conversations. He had just started, and I was on my way out to another job in a different location. The last conversation we had before I left, I thought for sure this was the day he would ask for my number and the elevator came to his floor and he got off but was still talking and trying to hold the elevator doors but the doors closed anyway. I didn't run into him after that. Now I can laugh about it but I was kind of sad at the time that I wouldn't see things through with this guy, unbeknownst to me this guy had quite the shady past, one involving domestic violence, which I find out months later. Now here I was not happy about not "running into him anymore" and God was over here keeping us separated for good reasons. Many times, God does not bring what we want to pass because he already sees what will happen and if God is kind enough to tell you No, tell him thank you! Thank God for closed doors! Because God knows, what he was saving you from! There's no reason to lose faith in God or stop trusting him. Pride hinders our trust in God. Many have lost their lives, got into financial trouble, lost their jobs, their homes, or family because they wouldn't trust God with their lives. They thought they knew better than God and could do a better job. Let go of pride quick! It's one sin God hates, *Isaiah 2:12; Isaiah 23:9; James 4:6; Jeremiah 9:23; Proverbs 8:13; Proverbs 11:2; Proverbs 13:10.* Pride that keeps you from trusting God and relying on him, won't take you far in life, and eventually it will destroy you.

    I had to let God take control, and although it was not an easy process because I was still trying to hold on to some control. God showed me time after time, I did not trust him. My reactions told on me all the time! For instance, I would have days I would be rebellious against God because "I" didn't get what "I" want and I would tell God, "I'm not reading the bible today" "I'm tired of praying if this is not working", or "I'm done with this." Silly me, sometimes before the day ended God pulled me back to my senses and I end up asking him for forgiveness for my behavior! Sometimes he would work it out what "I" wanted but differently or at a later date, then I end up feeling stupid for my childish behavior. In my relationship with God, he never lets me enjoy pouting for too long, and I am thankful for that! Sometimes I tell him "I want to scream, let me scream, cry and pout." "I want to be mad" and he's like "I don't think so, go humble yourself," ouch. I also noticed I had times I did not rely on him as I should, and I would not bring to his attention the little things that bothered me or little things I struggled with. For instance, if I felt annoyed about something or someone, I did not bring it to the Most High attention; I kept it to myself. However, in my journey with him, I learned he was the best person to talk with. Sometimes he would show me where I was wrong, or he wanted to reveal a person's character. I did not think he needed to be bothered about what should I eat, wear, where to live and just daily necessities in life.

However, as I learn to build my relationship and draw closer to him, I learned that *I needed to acknowledge him in everything I do, and everything I was thinking about, even if it seems little. God cares about every aspect of our lives.* Especially, with a situation requiring wisdom, understanding and guidance, we must turn to God and trust him with all of our issues not just the big ones. The Most High is our Father, and he will love and direct us. Would your Father let you go to work with pajamas on? I do not think so, so trust God with every detail of your life, even the little ones. When we do not learn to turn to God for help, we try to make things better by our own efforts, it rarely works out as we would like, but God got all the answers we need. Any decisions you make that require wisdom also requires God attention. **Don't be a wise guy and end up being pounded on by life.** Learn to humble yourself, be a student of God. Trusting the Most High with every detail of your life will help you have a deeper and meaningful relationship with him, just as it would make a relationship better in a marriage. When you trust your spouse or a friend doesn't the relationship flow better? It is no different with God. As you draw closer to him, trust him with everything that is going on. With trust comes commitment.

Trusting God

Chapter Key Points

- Trusting involves knowing someone's character and ability.

- There is no doubt in trust.

- Faith will help you execute trust.

- A decision must be made whether to trust God.

- You must surrender to God, let go and let God.

- Learn to trust God will all issues (Big & Small).

Trusting God

"Trust in God and do good; dwell in the land, and feed on his Faithfulness." ~ **Psalm 37:3**

Checklist

- Trust God no matter what.
- Have a flashback * *(remember what the Most High has done for you in the past, when you trusted him).*
- Read about men and women in the bible that put their trust in God.
- Find scriptures on trust, faith & belief and meditate on them to build up your trust in God.
- Read and study your bible.

Notepad

_____
_____
_____
_____
_____
_____
_____
_____
_____
_____
_____
_____

Trusting God

Scriptures to Meditate

~Psalm 31:14
"But as for me, I trust in you, O God; I say, "You are my Elohim."

~Nahum 1:7
"God is good, a stronghold in the day of trouble; and he knows those who trust in him."

~Jeremiah 17:7
"Blessed is the man who trust in God, and whose hope is Elohim."

~Psalm 118:8
"It is better to trust in the God than to put confidence in man."

~Psalm 125:1
"Those who trust in the God are like Mount Zion, which cannot be moved, but abides forever."

MILLY J

Trusting God

Prayer

In the name of Yahshua, I decide today to trust you and lean not on my understanding. I realize by trusting you, I remain in your protection, blessing, wisdom and guidance. Everything I need is in you. Therefore, I will trust in you and not my own abilities or man's abilities. I trust you in good times and in bad times. I know and believe you love me and will never leave me or forsake me. Amen.

TAKING STEPS TO DRAW CLOSER TO GOD

• CHAPTER 3 •

Making A Commitment

"Delight yourself in God and he shall give you the desire of your heart. Commit your way to Elohim, trust also in him, and he shall bring it to pass."

~Psalm 37:4-5

If you thought trusting was difficult, try making a commitment! Today failed relationships are perfect examples on how hard making a commitment can be. However, making a commitment is necessary to draw closer to God. Just as the sun is committed to the sky, God requires the same constant commitment from you. Your commitment to God does not change because you got married, you move out of the country; you are a single parent, you're a full-time student, you're too young, or you have too much things to do.

How many times have you been in a committed relationship? How many of these committed relationships were you fully committed? In addition, what happened when you made a commitment on your end but the other party did not? How did you feel? Did you feel betrayed? Or confuse? Hurt? Unloved? Now think about how the Most High feels when he has made a commitment to you, but you have not committed yourself to him. When you decide to be committed to God, this includes in every way, not just volunteering at church. Your commitment means you are honoring him with your life, your situations, and your family and not just with your words but with your actions. It means to respect his will for your life even if it differs from what "you prefer." It means being faithful and living according to his word. *Commitment is being faithful to God.* Your faithfulness will determine how much of a commitment you will make to the Most High. *Being faithful is being loyal and consistent.* Have you ever meant an un-loyal person? How did you view this person? Do you want God to look at you as an un-loyal follower? Loyalty is important when making a commitment, *Proverbs 20:6*. A commitment to God also involves trusting and committing to something in the present and future. It is a pledge and a promise to do something now and later.

A commitment to the Most High is like a commitment to marriage. In fact, to help you further understand the importance of committing to God, I want you to see yourself as his bride instead of just a believer, because the church is his bride, *Isaiah 54:5; Ephesians 5:25-27, 2 Corinthians 11:2; Revelation 19:7-9*. Now do not get dramatic and "spooky" here with this and have physical "wedding ceremonies," nowhere in the bible God instructed us to have physical wedding ceremonies marrying him or his Son, that is a fabricated concept, it is not biblical. The only marriages that took place in the bible were the ones involving two people who were present, *Genesis 2:20-24; Mark 10:6-9; Jeremiah 29:6; Genesis 2:18; 1 Corinthians 11:3*. God does not take part nor enjoy foolishness, *1 Corinthians 2:14; Ephesians 5:1-7; Proverbs 18:2; Revelation 22:18. God marriage to the church is spiritual.* It may "seem" like a positive thing to have these wedding ceremonies but it is not biblical. That is why there is so much confusion in the church. Many people are sitting there creating these fabricated concepts because it "seems" like a "good" idea but it is not a God idea. Stop the spread of confusion; focus on what is true and biblical so you do not get yourself into trouble. Pray for a spirit of discernment so you can identify what is biblical and what is not. Many that are doing these things are marrying "Jesus" on Saturday and going on dates on Sunday. Wouldn't that be adultery? Riddle me this, when you meet your spouse in the flesh how are you going to explain to Jesus that you are marrying another man? Are you going to ask Jesus for a divorce? I'm pretty sure you can't say, "You're just playing" or "It wasn't a real wedding." How would that look to God you playing around with marriage like that? Don't put yourself in compromising positions. We get it, you want to show your devotion and commitment but the best way to show that is to submit to God's will. A ceremony won't change your actions if you haven't applied the word to your life. The comparison to marriage in the bible is for us to learn how serious God takes this relationship. There are things you would or should not do in a marriage and it is the same for our relationship with the Most High. As believers, we are called to live a specific life, a holy life. Although it may seem impossible, it is possible, but it will take a lot of hard work and making a commitment to God.

WHAT DOES IT MEAN TO BE COMMITTED TO GOD? *Making a commitment to God means turning away from what he does not want you to do and do what he wants you to do and doing it all the time.* Some people give up at this point. The Most High is about doing great things. He is not trying to take fun out of your life; he wants to give you life, *John 3:16*, so be encouraged. The decision you make to commit your life and your ways to God, means you are deciding to surrender to him and do what he wants you to do and not what you want to do. **Committing** *your life to the Most High is about giving him authority to change your thinking and actions and replacing it with his thinking and actions and remember he thinks higher than we do, Isaiah 55:9.* For example, one of the Most High greatest commandments is to love God with all your heart, mind, and soul and love thy neighbor as you love yourself, if you commit to him; you also are deciding to obey that commandment. I know this is difficult, but it is one of God requirements and commandment. In fact, in *1 John 4:11* says, **"God so loved us, we also ought to love one another."** I know people make it difficult, but be encouraged, and understand we are all working on our love walk towards one another. It's one commandment we have to work harder on. I believe one day we will "get it."

Another example, is when you get married, you make a commitment to one another to be with only each other for life. You had to give up something and commit to your spouse. Committing to God is the same concept. Give up your ways of doing things and do things his ways. Now please understand the Most High is not talking about giving up on all your goals and dreams and becoming a nun. When we commit to him, in return he is asking us to give up all the bad, sinful, wicked behaviors and thinking we have for his righteousness. He desires to mold us to better people. Committing to him will develop your character, help build your faith in him and grow you spiritually. Making a commitment to God requires making a choice because a double-minded man is unstable in his ways, *James 1:8.*

Commitment also requires consistency to work. *When you commit to God, either you are in or you are out. There is no compromising with God. You can't offer God alternatives.* You can't say to God "If you do this, then I'll do that," It won't work. I tried it! God response to your offer will be these and then some, *John 14:15; Hebrews 10:26; James 4:17; Joshua 24:14-15; 2 John 1:7-11; Matthew 6:24; 1 Chronicles 10:13-14; Isaiah 1:18-20; Romans 6:1-4; James 4:4; Galatians 5:9; Proverbs 14:12.* After reading these scriptures I guarantee you, you won't be asking God for a compromise. If you examine *Psalm 37:4-5* scripture notice one promise of committing to the Most High, is that he will give you the desires of your heart; that is what "good" desire you have in your heart; he wants to give it to you. However, it involves making a commitment.

Make a commitment to reading and studying your bible, executing what you have read in the bible, and applying it to your life, being doers of the word and not just hearers, *James 1:22-23*. Take all the steps to draw closer to him. In order for you to see the importance of committing to God, ask yourself, what else is more important? Commitments are difficult, but what can you accomplish if you do not make a commitment to something? And why not to the Most High? I cannot think of any other way you can go around not making a commitment to God. If you want to learn about commitment, start with him. When you can commit to God, you will also enable yourself to make commitments to other important relationships, such as a marriage and business partnerships. *Commitments require time, effort, patience and determination. If you can handle the challenges of committing to God, you can do anything.* Decide what your goals are in drawing closer to God and act on that decision by taking the necessary steps to change. For instance, when you set yourself to accomplish a goal, you make a commitment to see it through, God is asking for the same commitment. The bible instructs us, what he wants us to do, *1 John 2:15-17*.

The book of Romans is also a great place to learn about life with God, read it, study it, meditate on it, and live it. Take the time to read the bible and get an understanding what the Most High is asking of you. It will not be easy, but it will be necessary. Renewing your mind will aid you in committing to God. As you renew your mind with God's word (the bible), your thinking will line up with his word, and your heart will be receptive to his ways and committing to him will not be an issue for you. Drawing closer to the Most High will become much easier when you make a commitment to him as you renew your mind. Renewing your mind involves reading the word of God and living out the word. *Romans 12:1-2* says, *"I beseech you therefore, brethren, by the mercy of God, that you present your bodies as a living sacrifice, holy and pleasing to God, which is your reasonable service. And do not conform to this world, but be "transformed by the renewing of your mind, that you may prove what is good and acceptable and perfect will of God."* It is God's will we do not conform to this world but be transformed with his word. We are a living sacrifice. We are his representatives on earth. Living out the word in your life will not be easy. You will be challenged, tested and will sometimes feel guilt over not being able to do everything like the bible instructed. However, he knows we will struggle because of our nature. If you rely on him to guide you, you will come to the place God wants and needs you to be.

Committing to God cannot be done with a nonchalant attitude either, Yahshua states in *Luke 14:27 "And whoever does not bear his cross and come after me cannot be my disciple."* That is a major statement about loyalty and being committed to God. Are you prepared to make the word of God your final authority, especially when others come against you or question your belief? Are you willing to not sin? Are you ready to serve God and only him, putting down your idols? Are you willing to give up on what "you think is right" for what he says is right? These are some things God will require of you as part of your commitment to him. The good news is he will help you prepare. When you get in his word and read the bible, you are preparing yourself to make a commitment to the Most High. You will see everything he requires of you, and all the benefits of committing to him. So do not fear no worries here! Pray about committing to the Most High and watch him bring it to pass. Pray.

Making A Commitment

Chapter Key Points

- Being committed to God is giving him authority over your thinking and actions.

- Commitment is being faithful and loyal to God and his word.

- Renewing your mind will help you in committing to God ways of doing things.

- Drawing closer to God becomes easier as you become more and more committed to him.

- Committing to God requires time, patience, determination and requires consistency to work.

Making A Commitment

"Into your hand I commit my spirit; you have redeemed me, O Elohim of truth." ~ **Psalm 31:5**

Checklist

- Commit to God.
- Understand what making a commitment to the Most High requires: **Romans 12:1-2.**
- Act on that decision.
- Read and study your bible.
- Pray.

Notepad

_____
_____
_____
_____
_____
_____
_____
_____
_____
_____
_____

Making A Commitment

Scriptures to Meditate

~Ephesians 5:17

"Therefore do not be unwise, but understand what the will of the God is."

~Psalm 119:33

"Teach me, O Elohim, the way of your statutes, and I shall keep it to the end."

~Proverbs 16:3

"Commit your works to God, and your thoughts will be Established."

~Psalm 119:101
"I have restrained my feet from every evil way, that I may keep your word."

MILLY J

Making A Commitment

Prayer

Yahweh, today and forever more, I make a commitment to follow your ways and obey your word. I lay down my plans and thoughts for yours Elohim. I know it will not be easy, but thank you for the Holy Spirit who will guide and instruct me. I am willing and ready to make a commitment to you. I can do all things through Yahshua who strengthens me. Amen.

TAKING STEPS TO DRAW CLOSER TO GOD

• CHAPTER 4 •

Learning to Pray

"But you, when you pray, go into your room, and when you have shut your door, pray to your Father who is in the secret place, and your Father who sees in secret will reward you openly."

~Matthew 6:6

Have you ever been confused about a situation in your life and when you prayed about it, you felt better? Likewise, you felt not only better, you also felt closer to God? Prayer is another step to drawing closer to God. There are many benefits to prayer. First, you build and strengthen your relationship with him. Second, prayer changes situations around and provides the answers to your questions. Third, it takes out the stress of thinking you are on your own. Fourth, God wants us to pray, *"Be anxious for nothing, but in everything by prayer and supplication, with thanksgiving, let your requests be made known to God; and the peace of God, which surpasses all understanding, will guard your hearts and minds through Yahshua," Philippians 4:6-7*. Fifth, prayer builds up your spiritual life, your faith and trust in the Most High. Last, the peace of God comes over you when you pray.

The scripture above, **Matthew 6:6**, is a great scripture to meditate on, let us examine it. The Most High is saying since you took the time to seek and prayed to him, he will reward you for that. He will reward you for drawing closer to him. Prayer is your communication time with the Most High. In all relationships you will have, communication will be key. When you lack communication, you lack a relationship. In fact, communication problems are one of many reasons many people cannot get along with each other. Many friendships and marriages become strain because of communication problems. We lack the ability to communicate our true feelings with people and because of this; we may feel inadequate to communicate with the Most

High. However, to draw closer to God, you must communicate with him. The Most High communicates with us daily and if you pay attention, you will notice his communication is in the form of love. When you embrace that, I believe it will help you open up to him, and will help you communicate with others better. When we pray to God, we are communicating and saying to him, *"God I receive your love for me and I want to take part in this relationship."* He wants that from us. He longs to be your friend, and Father. Whatever you need him to be; he wants to be that for you. So pray, talk with him, let him know what you are thinking, and how you are feeling.

Men are often taught to suppress their emotions at an early age. If they express kindness, they are seen as "weak." If they express strength, they are seen as "aggressive." Although, society won't let you express your emotions, **God will and wants his man of God to yield to him.** There is nothing wrong for a woman or a man to express what they are feeling. It's unfair to allow one to express themselves and be emotional and then put down another for doing the same. If you submit yourself to God, then you shouldn't be bottling up any emotions because with God, you can tell him how hurt you are, the pain you feel and he will not judge you and prayer time is a perfect place to do that. My circle is small and there is only one hand full of people I can trust to communicate with but when it comes to communicating with God, I let it all out. God always answer back and you may not hear him in an audible voice but in your spirit, he will speak to you.

FINDING YOUR SECRET PLACE You should make daily prayer a part of your life. God is ready to give answers and guide us every day. You do not have to wait until something bad happens to pray, pray daily, **Luke 18:1**. You should not have a lukewarm spirit regarding prayer in your life either, **James 5:16**. Prayer is important if you want to draw closer to the Most High. Take the time to read about Yahshua ministry in the New Testament, he mostly prayed. If Yahshua, the Son of the God can take the time to pray, there is no excuse why you cannot do the same. Just remember times in your life, when you didn't pray, didn't you feel you were far from God? Didn't you feel you can't change the situation? Or that life was spinning out of control and you had no hiding place? That is why the scripture say, "Go into your secret room." The secret room is your safe place.

I believe Yahshua spent so much time in prayer because he knew people who would betray, accuse, and would kill surrounded him. He knew only the Most High could give him the strength to deal with the world. Do you know even when you are helping others; it can take a lot from your strength? However, when you pray daily, the stress of being pulled here and there will disappear, because you recognize your source comes from above. That is why prayer is so important. **Prayer is power**. God will energize us through prayer and give us peace. We can come to him and pray knowing he hears us and will answer our prayers based on his will for our lives. While you pray, you will feel the Most High and his peace surrounding you. He desires to be near to us, but only if we allow him to be. When you understand the importance of prayer and why it's necessary to draw closer to God, you will be blessed. Daily prayer will not be a challenge or chore for you; instead, it will be a blessing. Praying should not feel stressful or bothersome to you. Each time you take the time to pray to the Most High, you are saying to him, *"I love you God, I desire to be near to you, I want to draw closer to you,"* and he desires the same. **Never look at prayer as a waste of time. It is one of the most important times because only you and God are connecting.**

You might ask yourself, well how should I pray? I do not know how to pray. *Matthew 6:6-13* tells us how we can pray, *"But you, when you pray, go into your room, and when you have shut your door, pray to your Father who is in the secret place; and your Father who sees in secret will reward you openly. And when you pray, do not use vain repetitions as the heathen do. For they think they will be heard for their many words. Therefore, do not be like them. For your Father knows the things you have need of before you ask Him. In this manner, therefore pray: Our Father in Heaven, hallowed be your name. your kingdom come. Your will be done on earth as it is in Heaven. Give us this day our daily bread. And forgive us our debts, as we forgive our debtors. And do not lead us into temptation, but deliver us from the evil one. For yours is the kingdom and the power and the glory forever. Amen."* This kind of prayer tells us you do not have to complicate your prayer life. If you are praying in line with God word, which is his will, that is all you need. One example of praying in God word is this: "Father I thank you are supplying all my needs according to your riches in glory by Yahshua," this prayer is based on *Philippians 4:19* scripture. Therefore, if you do not know what to pray about, add scriptures to your prayers. The Most High said his word never return to him void, *Isaiah 55:11*. There is no need to be dramatic. The most powerful prayers I have prayed came directly from the scriptures. Keep in mind that day to day, your prayers will change; there is no routine for praying. Today you might pray for healing, the next day you're praying for peace. Pray what is in your heart. Nothing can be hidden from God, so let it out.

It is important to find a place to pray. Yahshua always found his secret place, prayed and spent time with God quietly, *Matthew 26:38-39; Luke 6:12; Luke 5:16; Matthew 14:23; Mark 1:35*. I encourage you to find the time and a quiet place to communicate (pray) with God daily. Give him all the details of what is going on in your life. He desires to comfort you. I know some of you may not have a "quiet place" or at least you think you don't, but there is a time in your day you are alone, whether it's in the bathroom, in the shower, at lunch time, in the break room, in your car, when everyone goes to bed, there is a time when it can become your secret place, take advantage of that time. One way I spend time with God in my secret place is during Sabbath. One thing I love about the Sabbath and doing it, is shutting down. When I do my Sabbath, the television is turned off during that time, I do not take calls or make calls that day, the phone is off. I use the computer because I watch my Sabbath online, but once that is done, the computer goes off and I concentrate my time in studying my bible, praying, praising and worshiping God right in my living room! I call it my "Shut-down Day."

Many will called the Sabbath "Old Testament" thinking but I believe it is still relevant to practice today because it forces you to recognize what matters. The time I spend focusing on God energizes me. I love being unplugged from the world even if it is for a few hours. I feel renewed, loved, and rested. During those times, God reveals more spiritual truth to me because there is no noise coming in from the outside. God appreciates us being with him whether it is on the Sabbath or any other day. I believe there is a reason he mentions keeping the Sabbath as a commandment, *Isaiah 58:13-14*. I don't believe it is done with because if that was the case then all the commandants would have to be done with, and that can never be the case and some will argue that the commandants have been reduced to two things, found in *Matthew 22:37-40*. However, just because the commandants been reduced does not mean you can take the name of God (Yahweh) in vain (Second Commandment), or go around killing others (Fifth Commandment) or have other gods before him (First Commandment), disrespect your parents (Fourth Commandment), you're still following the same ten commandant reduced to two, follow that logic, *Matthew 5:17-20*. In addition, those with the arguments still cannot tell you what is wrong with setting a day focusing on God and resting in him? What kind of pastor would tell you it is wrong to rest and block time to spend with God whether it is for Sabbath or any other day? *Colossians 2:16 says* *"So let no one judge you in food or drink, or regarding a festival or a new moon or Sabbaths, which are a shadow of things to come, but the substance is of Yahshua."*

At the end of the day, it is about God, so before you shun Sabbath away based on what you may have heard, know it was not a mistake that God made it the third commandment. Now I am not here to tell you what day you should spend with God or get "unplugged" that is up to you. Every day is a good day to spend with God; you are not limited to one day of the week, and God is not limited to one day of the week. God wants to communicate with us daily. I am just sharing my personal experience with you. You can go to church every day if you like. I inadvertently attended a nondenominational church on Saturday nights for nine years, so I became a custom to spending my Saturdays with God. That doesn't mean I can't go to church on Monday, or Friday or Wednesday. Where I live, I don't have the Sabbath teaching I feel will grow me, so I watch one online at home, but I don't mind going to church to fellowship with other believers, and enjoy praise and worship service. I don't think God will be upset about you seeking him and wanting to spend time with him on any day. Only human beings find issues with days, times, and focuses and find problems with what others are doing because they are not doing it, *Romans 14:5*. What is important, is how God is viewing it, not humankind. Disputing about days, times and hours doesn't grow you spiritually and contribute nothing to the kingdom of God. Focus on what matters-your relationship with God.

WHAT ABOUT UNANSWERED PRAYERS? One issue I know I struggled with about praying and I know many others do also, is when you prayed and fasted and the opposite happens or your prayer is not answered. How frustrating is that! Sometimes I get discourage and mad, but then God speaks to my heart to humble me. I can give you many reasons your prayer "might not" have been answered but one thing I know for sure only God knows the reason he did not answer it. Sometimes he will reveal the reason to you, sometimes years later and sometimes never but do not let unanswered prayers stop you from communicating with God because doing so will harden your heart.

I know it is difficult to be believing, waiting, trusting, hoping, only for it not to happen but believe God has a reason. *Many times his reasons are not what we can understand physically but what we come to understand spiritually.* I had many prayers that either was not answered or have yet to be answered, some as long as 14 years has passed, with no answer! However, no matter how "I" ended feeling not seeing the results, I did not stop praying. I also had many prayers answered, so I know God hears me. It is just a matter of his timing and whether what I'm praying about is in his will for my life. I cannot force him to answer me, I trust he knows best. I want to encourage you, not to give up on prayer if you are face or have faced a challenging situation and you felt God ignore you because that is not the case. *Nothing is more humbly than not getting want you want and finding out later it was a blessing in disguise you did not get it,* so do not give up on God or your prayers. God has higher plans for you, *"For I know the thoughts I think toward you, says* GOD, *thoughts of peace and not of evil, to give you a future and a hope. Then you will call upon me, go, and pray to me, and I will listen to you. And you will seek me and find me when you search for me with all your heart," Jeremiah 29:11-13.*

I want to remind you to be mindful of what you are praying for whether your prayers are to get back at someone who did you wrong, or praying for "increase" of material possessions. It seem like many churches are focused on getting you to have a "millionaire" or "billionaire" mindset. I understand the need for coming out of poverty. Poverty is a spirit that seeks to keep you down so you won't achieve your best in life. Some argue that poverty is "humbly," however, I don't know how humble someone can be if they are starving to death or they are facing eviction or they have to get "generic" medical treatment because they can't afford good medical care. Poverty is not good and not fun. Some ways I see poverty can be humbling is if you once experience it and came out of it and now you appreciate what God has provided for you or you come to realize material gain is not gain at all if you sell your soul. However, poverty that keeps you depending on others, or the government for basic needs, can't be a good thing. I'm not an advocate for poverty and I'm not an advocate on focusing on only money either.

There are plenty of people with money who are miserable and we all die whether rich or poor. A rich person can't escape death neither can a poor person. We can all be in spiritual poverty, which I think is probably worst, as this separate us from God.

I also want to encourage you to stop wasting time praying for mansions, the latest car, and millions of dollars. *"Do not love the world or the things in the world. If anyone loves the world, the love of the Father is not in him,"* (1 John 2:15-17). Learn to be content, *"Let your conduct be without covetousness; be content with such things as you have. For he himself has said, I will never leave you nor forsake you,"* (Hebrews 13:5). You can also read more on contentment in *Philippians 4:11-13; Matthew 6:31-33; Psalm 16:8-11; Proverbs 16:8; and Luke 12:22-34.* These same people and leaders that are promoting praying to be rich have fallen into a snare and they might not realize it and you entering the same snare. They are never content and will always desire more and ask more from you, *"He who loves silver (money) will not be satisfied with silver (money); nor he who loves abundance, with increase. This also is vanity,"* (Ecclesiastes 5:10). Now you see why the rich get richer, the thought of not having more than enough money, drives them crazy and many develop the spirit of greed. For those in the church body the scripture tells us *"Likewise deacons must be reverent, not double-tongued, not given too much wine, not greedy for money, holding the mystery of the faith with a pure conscience,"* (1 Timothy 3:8-9) and this applies to all of us not just deacons.

Some will try to convince you it is biblical to pray for riches, and that so and so was rich but do not disclose that so and so was rich but they weren't praying to be rich, they weren't praying for cars, and mansions and more money, God blessed them, that is a big difference. Abraham was rich in cattle, gold and silver, **Genesis 13:2**, that is true; Job was one of the richest man in the East, **Job 1:1-3**. It is all true they were rich and many other people in the bible were also rich; Joseph, David, Solomon, Isaac, and it's true that God can bless you with wealth.

The ones, who prayed for prosperity and blessings, prayed it humbling not for "appearance" to say they succeeded in life, or to walk around puff up because they are "rich" and feel like they are untouchable. They weren't praying specifically "God bless me with 100 million cattle's so I can be the greatest farmer on earth for all to see." They were not praying, "God give me 10,000 acre of land so I can build a mansion." They prayed a general prayer that opens the door to God blessing them with not just wealth, but healing, wisdom, knowledge and spiritual growth. King Solomon prayed for prosperity for the people, **Psalm 72** and Jabez prayed for God to enlarge his territory, *1 Chronicles 4:10*. However, let us look at what Jabez said in his prayer, *1 Chronicles 4:10* **"And Jabez called on the Elohim of Israel saying, "Oh, that you would bless me indeed, and enlarge my territory, that your hand would be with me, and that you would keep me from evil, that I may not cause pain!, "So God granted him what he requested."** Jabez was humbled in his prayer, he not only ask for an increase in blessings but he asked God to keep him from evil, that God hands be on him and that He may not cause pain, because he knew the more you gain the more you lose your mind and with God hands on him he will be directed by the Most High on how to handle his increase of blessings. He knew his prayer require God hands and God to be first. In addition, don't be so quick in thinking when he prayed for his territory to be enlarge that it meant something for monetary value, it could be he was asking the Most High to enlarge his influence in the kingdom. Maybe he was planning on building an orphanage on the land. If you are praying for a mansion, whom other than you and your family will this mansion bless? Will you be taking in orphan children, or people who are homeless to live in there as well? If you lose your home, will your pastor open their mansion to you? Will your leader give you a plane ride if you needed to go to England for medical treatment? Probably not.

When you are praying, be humble and honest about what you are asking. Are you even ready to receive it? I understand the desire for nice things, but do not let that be what you pray for. Stay focus; praying about the right things, like increase in wisdom; like Solomon did in **1 Kings 3:5**-14 and understanding, spiritual insight, and leave the rest to God! When we take the time to seek him and his ways first, that promise will be fulfilled. God is not taking anything away from you, but instead his adding to you. When you place other priorities first instead of God, it will be difficult for you to draw closer to him. As you pray, praise, give thanks and worship the Most High. When you finish praying, don't just rush up and go about your business, take a few minutes and be still to hear him speak to you, *Psalm 46:10.* Use your prayer time to draw closer to God. Take the time to experience his peace and love.

TAKING STEPS TO DRAW CLOSER TO GOD

Learning to Pray

Chapter Key Points

- God wants us to pray, **Philippians 4:6-7**.

- Prayer allows you to communicate with God.

- Prayer strengthens your relationship with God.

- Prayer is power.

- Prayer can be used to draw closer to God.

MILLY J

Learning to Pray

"Pray without ceasing"
~ 1 Thessalonians 5:17

Checklist

- Understand the reasons for praying.
- Get scriptures from the bible and pray them.
- Find scriptures on prayer and meditate on them.
- Find and take the time to pray.
- After praying be still and hear God speak to you.

Notepad

_____
_____
_____
_____
_____
_____
_____
_____
_____

TAKING STEPS TO DRAW CLOSER TO GOD

Learning to Pray

Scriptures to Meditate

~Ephesians 6:18
"Praying always with all prayer and supplication in the Spirit, being watchful to this end with all perseverance and supplication for all the saints."

~Philippians 4:6
"Be anxious for nothing, but in everything by prayer and supplication, with thanksgiving, let your requests be made known to God."

~Luke 11:2-4
"So he said to them, 'When you pray, say: Our Father in Heaven, hallowed be your name. Your kingdom come. Your will be done on earth as it is in Heaven. Give us day by day our daily bread. And forgive us our sins, for we also forgive everyone who is indebted to us. And do not lead us into temptation, but deliver us from the evil one."

~Psalm 4:1
"Hear me when I call, O Elohim of my righteousness! You have relieved me in my distress; have mercy on me, and hear my prayer."

~Matthew 21:22
"And whatever things you ask in prayer, believing, you will receive."

MILLY J

Learning to Pray

Prayer

Yahweh, I desire to communicate with you through my prayers. I long to hear you speak to me and instruct me. I pray that your word be my daily bread. Teach me to pray, oh Elohim. I believe your ears are open to hear my prayers. I believe when I pray, my prayers are answered; therefore I will not be anxious for nothing. I pray that you help me stay focus on you and your goodness. I thank you that your will be done in my life. Amen.

TAKING STEPS TO DRAW CLOSER TO GOD

• CHAPTER 5 •

The Greatest Commandment

"And above all these put on love, which binds everything together in perfect harmony."

~ Colossians 3:14 (ESV)

LOVE? What does love have to do with this? The first thing to learn about the Most High is that he is love and everything he does is base on love. Understand that God loves you and wants the best for you. When I was a little girl I never doubted God love for me, I had a natural reverence for him even when I did not completely comprehend him as a child, but I knew he was always watching over me. God loves you no matter who you are, where you come from, and what you do. You must understand that his love is not base on emotions or conditions. As human beings, we are often use to loving others based on our emotions, which involves loving someone "because." God love is different. His love is unconditional and similar to a parent's love towards their children. God will love you through your difficulties, your sinning days, and your holy days. He may not like everything we do, but his love is unwavering. God love is available to you. Even if you never experienced love with another human being, when you understand God love for you, you will see that there is no comparison. Because he is love, love will be needed.

God desire love towards him. He requires us to love him, with all our heart, mind and soul, *Luke 10:27* that is his first and greatest commandment. To draw closer to the Most High, you got to love. Be love and give love. If you do not have love in your heart, especially towards the things of God, it will be difficult for you to draw closer to him. Love will be the reason that all the steps I shared with you will work in your life. Your behavior and thoughts towards the Most High will determine how much you love him. Will you ignore him to do what is pleasing to you, even when it is the wrong thing? We show our love towards God, through our obedience to his word. The more you show him you love him through your actions, the fewer issues you will have in obeying him and the word (the bible), **Psalm 97:10**.

So, how do you develop love for the things of God? You must first access where your heart is, **Matthew 6:21**. Whatever you treasure and made important in your life that is where your heart will be. If you treasure God and his word, then your heart will be with him, and love will be in you. When you are in love with God and his ways of doing things, seeking him will not be an issue, trusting him will not be an issue, committing to him will not be an issue, praying will not be an issue. Therefore, develop a love for the Most High and his righteousness and all these steps will work in your life. You will accomplish your goal to draw closer to him.

1 Corinthians 13 is the love chapter, and this chapter describes everything about love, meditate on it, read it, until it resonate in your spirit and becomes a part of you. Doing so, will help you check yourself when you are being selfish or hateful. For me the scripture *1 Corinthians 13:4-7* helps me stay in my love walk, especially when dealing with difficult people. We all know and have dealt with "difficult people" that make you feel you need to withdraw your love from them, but we have to rise higher than their behavior. I always remind myself, what if God withdrew his love from me how I would feel. It would devastate me, so I would not want someone else to feel devastated. Sometimes we have to love someone in the distance until they comprehend what love is. God does the same, he doesn't stand in the distance, but he waits for us to change our behavior, come out of sin, and come back to him. Throughout the bible, you'll find God pleaded with the people to come back to his bosom and receive his love and instructions. Receive the love God has for you and share that love with someone else.

Love is a two-way street, many people want love but refuse to give it back or they abuse your love. *1 Corinthians 13:4-7 (NIV)* says, *"Love is patient, love is kind. It does not envy, it does not boast, it is not proud. It does not dishonor others, it is not self-seeking, it is not easily angered, and it keeps no record of wrongs. Love does not delight in evil but rejoices with the truth. It always protects, always trusts, always hopes, and always perseveres."* I can't tell you countless of times where I hear people cry about not being loved back and ignore verse 4-7, it applies both ways. You can't be abusing someone's love and expect them to constant feed you love and for them not to get frustrated. If you love that person, verse 4-7 applies both ways, no exception!

What tickles me as well are those who do evil things to you and want you to love them through their evilness, the verses are clear" **Love does not delight in evil.**" You can't be evil to a person and think they should love you beating on them, cheating on them, robbing them, lying on them or destroying them. If you love then you cannot be evil, period! Many will argue that you are to "love" your enemies. Loving your enemy's means not treating them like they are treating you and not everyone fall under the title "enemy." Remember those who rise against you as "enemies" are often the devil's puppet, it's not really them working against you. It is an evil spirit that rises in them to come against you. That is why it is advised to "bind the devil" when praying. You can bind any evil spirit that is in someone. For example, if you have a cousin who uses drugs and every time you try to help them they go back to the drugs and robbed you, some church teaches you, you're supposed to keep being robbed to help that person, but what good is that? Instead, you need to be on your knees praying for that spirit, that drug demon to leave that person, and then you can help them. While the person is possessed with that demonic spirit, they can't receive from you because they can't comprehend what you are trying to do. They are not in their right mind. The definition of possess is "have complete power over," "hold as property," "own." Remember Yahshua had to cast out the demons because the demons were blocking the person from functioning normal.

Do you recall the little boy in **Mark 9:17-29**, he was possessed and that spirit in him was a mute spirit. The disciples weren't able to cast the demons out but when Yahshua got to him, he was able to do so. Then the disciples asked him, how come we couldn't do the same and Yahshua replied, **"This kind cannot be driven out by anything but prayer and fasting."** You can't pat the demon on the back and think you going to get good results. Medication doesn't work on demons either. It's a spiritual battle first then you can address the physical, *Ephesians 6:12*. We have to learn to identify whom our true enemy is- Satan. I don't love the devil, anything in his likeness, act like him or anything that represent him and he is my biggest enemy! The devil is your biggest enemy and God is not saying to love him at all! God is not saying for us to love evil either, because he himself said he hates evil, *Psalm 5:4-5; Proverbs 6:16-19; Proverbs 8:13; Psalm 97:10; Amos 5:15; Romans 12:9*. So don't let people confuse you with the "love your enemies" scripture, it doesn't apply to everything. *Some people want to be evil to hurt others and expect you to love them and treat them like they are not evil, they become our enemies because they choose to side with the devil.* The real enemy is the devil and there will be no love for him from a believer! Can you imagine loving evil?

Always remember that God loves you. No one will love you like God will. A man or woman may tell you "they are the only one that can love you" but that is not true. God is the only one that can love you, through your mess, your good and bad times. He knows you. He created you, so he knows how to love you. Let no one or any bad circumstance affect your ability to see and understand how much God loves you and wants the best for you. Love him by seeking him, obeying and trusting his will for your life. The Most High is all about doing great things. He will take you to a higher way of thinking that will bless you. Do not be afraid or intimidated. He values you. You are worthy, loved and accepted in his eyes. No matter how others may have treated you, or what they may have said about you, God loves you and accepts you. Seek, trust, commit, pray and love the Most High. He is expecting and waiting for you to experience his love and draw closer to him, will you respond? He is waiting with open arms to receive you in his bosom. Do you want to enter the bosom of the Most High and embrace his love for you?

The Greatest Commandment

Chapter Key Points

- Know God loves you no matter what.

- God requires us to love him with all our hearts, mind and soul.

- Access where your heart is concerning God and the things of God, **Matthew 6:21**, so these steps can work in your life.

The Greatest Commandment

"Love does no harm to a neighbor; therefore love is the fulfillment of the law" ~ ***Romans 13:10***

Checklist

- Understand and know God loves you.
- How will you show God how much you love him?
- Find and meditate on scriptures about love to learn about God's love.
- Practice your love walk-be love and show love to others- Stay in the circle of love.

Notepad

_____
_____
_____
_____
_____
_____
_____
_____
_____
_____
_____
_____
_____

MILLY J

The Greatest Commandment

Scriptures to Meditate

~Galatians 5:22

"But the fruit of the Spirit is love, joy, peace, long suffering, kindness, goodness, faithfulness."

~Ephesians 3:17

"That Yahshua may dwell in your hearts through faith; that you, being rooted and grounded in love."

~Colossians 2:2

"That their hearts may be encouraged, being knit together in love, and attaining to all riches of the full assurance of understanding, to the knowledge of the mystery of God, both of the Father and of Yahshua."

~1 John 4:7

"Beloved, let us love one another, for love is of God; and everyone who loves is born of God and knows God."

~John 3:16

"For God so loved the world that he gave his only begotten Son, that whoever believes in him should not perish but have everlasting life."

The Greatest Commandment

Prayer

Yahweh, I now know and understand your great love for me, thank you for loving me. I love you with all my heart, mind and soul and I will love my neighbors as I love myself. Thank you for your everlasting love, your unconditional love, I receive it in my life right now. I pray that your love shines through me and when people see me, they see love. I am love and I give love. Amen.

MILLY J

• CHAPTER 6 •

A Period of Testing

"Be sober; be vigilant; because your adversary the devil walks about like a roaring lion, seeking whom he may devour,"

~ *1 Peter 5:8*

TAKING STEPS TO DRAW CLOSER TO GOD

Drawing closer to God will not be a walk in the park. I want to warn you, in everything you will do to draw closer to God, there will be a period of testing and opposition. Many of us were saved in the church and you heard the sermons, accepted the call to confess Yahshua, left church happy and praising then the test comes and you're losing it. Some churches forget to tell you the battle is on now. You have entered the battlefield where Satan and his demons will come against you. The devil is not rejoicing over your decision to draw closer to the Most High, and he will do everything in his power to delay, distract, confuse, and stop you. The devil will make you think you are too busy, you do not need God, you're in control of your own life, or you are not perfect enough. He will make you think you have time later, but do not be fooled, tomorrow is not guaranteed, **James 4:14**. Don't be afraid either, but be encouraged, because Yahshua has already defeated him at the cross.

The most irony part about being saved is that God will also give you some exams. I know some of you may think, but why would God test me if I am doing all of this to get closer to him? Understand this, *everything you do for God will require faith, and nothing pleases him more than your faith, Hebrews 11:6*. God would love to give you everything you want, but are you ready for it? If you are going around saying how you want to draw closer to God, but never back up your words with actions, there is nothing he can do for you.

If you can't be faithful committing to God, reading, and studying your bible what reasons do you give him to trust and believe you want to be near him? He wants to see your commitment to him. He wants to see how far you will take your faith, *1 Peter 1:6-9*. God will examine you to see if you are faithful with the little things, like praying, reading your bible. Then he can trust you with bigger things; like praying and interceding for others, healing the sick, increasing the kingdom of God by spreading the gospel, *Luke 16:10-13, Matthew 25:23*. He will examine your heart and your faithfulness towards him and his word (the bible). Will what God says matter to you more than want you want to do or what everyone else is doing? The great news is that his exam period differs from the devil. When God examine us, he does this to increase us. We become mature and spiritual during and after a test.

Your faith, confidence, and trust in him will be strengthened. The devil tests you to destroy you and move you away from the will of God for your life, *John 10:10*. The devil goal is to see you disobey God word, as Adam and Eve did in the garden, *Genesis 3*, you must understand the difference. God will never tempt you or test you with evil things, *James 1:13; 1 Corinthians 10:13; Matthew 26:41*. However, when evil things come against you, he will watch to see how you will respond and he will help you, never forget that! However, he will watch to see if you will quit on him when things are upside down. Will you curse the ground you walk on, wishing you were never saved? Or never born? Or will you seek him for help? Or will you submit to the devil temptations?

Do you recall what happened to Job? Job was tested like no man had been tested before. Job experienced sickness, death, he lost his home, and repeatedly he was tested. His own wife told him to curse God, *Job 2:9*. Job had every reason to lose it and hate his life. Especially, since he did nothing wrong, he wasn't sinning, but God allowed him to be tested anyway. Job did not like what he was experiencing, none of us would. Did Job quit on God? He did not. He did not go sinning or gave up on God. He did not say to God, "Well since everything is going wrong for me anyway, let me go out there and tear it up, party over here, nothing over there." *Job did the opposite, and what was more humbling was that he submitted to the will of God, even when it was something terrible happening to him.* That humbled me because I be complaining about little stuff and get angry with God and here someone lost so much and still could submit to God's will. I felt I had so much to learn and work to do. The will of God for our life might not look like the gold road to Heaven, there will be thorns on your side on your way there, but God will take you through every adversity when we submit to him. At the end, Job was restored sevenfold of everything he lost, and God will do the same for you. He will restore you, strengthen you, and give you wisdom.

I encourage you to spend time in the Book of Job. It's also a good one to go back to when you feel you are being challenged more than you can bear. I always feel encouraged after reading the Book of Job because it snaps me right out of my bad attitude about my situation into yielding to God's will and becoming stronger spiritually, mentally and physically.

Many people fear the thought of going through any challenges, especially those involving death of loves ones, financial lost, and sickness but during God's exams, his grace and mercy will always be there to protect you. There is a maturing process under the Most High examination. Use the trials and tribulations to help mature you in the things of God. God speaks to us through our spirit so he has to test us to make sure we are spiritually equipped. Can you give the devil a beat down with a stick or do you have to access spiritual ways to beat him down, like praying and fasting? Logically, you will not be walking in your living room with a bat swinging talking about you will beat the devil and the demons out, no way! You will go into prayer, submitting to God, and fasting, *Ephesians 6:11-12* says *"Put on the whole armor of God, that you may stand against the wiles of the devil. For we do not wrestle against flesh and blood, but against principalities, against powers, against rulers of the darkness of this age, against spiritual hosts of wickedness in the heavenly place."* This is a spiritual battle not a physical one.

All of your emotional up and downs, depression, anger issues, or self-esteem issues, they are all demonic spirits attacking your mind spiritually, so you can't hit your head with a pan thinking the devil will come out, instead you submit to God and get in your bible, find scriptures concerning health, your mind, and apply them to your life, *Philippians 4:6-13; 2 Timothy 1:7;*

Psalm 91; Matthew 6:34; Romans 8:6. That is why the bible instructs us to "cast down imaginations and every high thing that exalt itself against the knowledge of God, and bringing into captivity every thought to the obedience of Yahusha," *2 Corinthians 10:5*. Captivity means to imprisoned. The devil is trying to imprison your mind, your spirit, your soul, and even your body with demonic spirits to hold you down and keep you away from God. You can't win a battle if you are using the wrong weapon.

As you draw closer to God and really get into bible study, God will reveal to you all the spiritual things happening around you. He will reveal people's true intentions to you. I have had times when someone is talking and the Holy Spirit is telling me that this person is being deceptive with me. The Holy Spirit has shown me people working against me because of their jealousy and envy. In the physical, I wouldn't have known this because these people are smiling in my face, giving me hugs yet they are plotting against me or hated me. You will sit in your corner, minding your business, not bothering anyone and people will still come against you. They will lie on you, cheat on you, take from you, talk bad about you, and create stories about you and the majority of the time they do not even know you. Some people are easily used by the devil because their spirit and heart is full of wickedness already, so they are in a perfect place to be the devil's puppet, *Matthew 12:35; Jeremiah 17:9; Mark 7:21-23; Romans 1:21*. You need God revelation and only God can reveal these spiritual things to you so you can prepare yourself in prayer. Your pastor can't reveal every details of your life to you, but God can. When God had revealed spiritual things to me, the scripture **"No weapon form against me shall prosper,"** from *Isaiah 54:17* had a new meaning. That was my heads up that even though someone will work against you; it will fail because God has your back! Now you need to be careful when God reveals something spiritual to you. You will have to learn to balance this out. You cannot go around with a "big head" thinking you know it all. You cannot go around abusing what God has revealed to you. Do not abuse others because of what you know. God will deal with you accordingly if you betray his trust. Do not go around calling yourself a "prophet or prophetess" if God has not told you this loud and clear. Most of the time, I share nothing with anyone concerning what God has revealed. Some things are truly between you and him and if he wants you to share it, he will let you know, until then put a tape on it.

    HOW CAN I PASS THE TEST? You need to be prepared for the warfare that the devil is preparing against you, *Ephesians 6:10-13*. The great news regarding these battles is that God has already declared your victory. So walk out that fiery furnace *Daniel 3:13-30*, jump out of the lions' den, *Daniel 6:16-24*! Would you like to know how to pass these tests? You pass the test, by first, obeying the word of God, *John 14:15*. When you read your bible, you'll see that everything he asks us to do is because it is for our own good and the good of others. He even tells us how we can pass the devil's test, in *James 4:7*, **"Therefore, submit to God, resist the devil and he will flee from you."** The devil will suggest many alternatives to you, but you must resist him. Submit to God instead of the devil. One way of resisting the devil, is to renew your mind to God's way of thinking, **Romans 12:2**. Another way is to apply scriptures to your situations and cast down the negative thoughts and images the devil tries to tempt you with, **2 Corinthians 10:3-5**. You know saying, "what would Yahshua do," live by it.

The devil will also use the sin you are still in to fight against you, so come out of whatever sin you are in, whether it's a little one or a big one. Having sin in your life will be the devil's first-class ticket to your plane. He might even become the pilot if you don't flee from sin. Here is where we need to humble ourselves; we are all sinners. I am a sinner, your pastor is a sinner, your children are sinners, yes even the newborn, your neighbor is a sinner and you are a sinner, **Psalm 51:5; Ecclesiastes 7:20; Romans 3:23; Romans 3:10; 1 John 1:10**. However, we do not have to stay being a sinner, we can come out of it through the word of God, and he shows us how. When many think of sin, they think of something bad they have done (their actions), but our thinking can be sinful, so you have to mindful of that when you are working to get rid of sin in your life. You are not alone; the Holy Spirit is your Helper yield to him. The Holy Spirit will direct you and warn you, **John 14:16-17; John 16:13; Galatians 5:22-23**. Do not ignore what the Holy Spirit has instructed you to do. To ignore the Holy Spirit, is to ignore God. The Holy Spirit is that inner voice, telling you something is not right, do this, or do not do that, listen to it. Pass the test!

PRACTICAL STEPS TO DRAW CLOSER TO GOD

- Rely on the word of God: *John 14:15; Luke 4:4.*

- Renew your mind: *Romans 12:1-2; Ephesians 4:23; Philippians 4:8-9.*

- Resist (the devil & temptations): *James 4:7; James 1:12; 2 Corinthians 10:3-5.*

- Put on your Armor: *Ephesians 6:11-18; Ephesians 4:22-24.*

- Be guided by the Holy Spirit: *John 14:26; John 16:13.*

TAKING STEPS TO DRAW CLOSER TO GOD

• CHAPTER 7 •

Test Your Self

"Let us test and examine our ways and return to Yahweh!"

~Lamentations 3:40

As you begin your journey in drawing closer to God, I want you to test yourself, your actions and thinking. Do they line up with the Most High? Many times as believers, we go through life as if anything and everything can happen to us, but that is not true. We can avoid many things if we take the time to test our spiritual lives. Ask yourself, why do certain things happen in my life? How can I make things better? Is there a hidden sin in my life? Have I been thinking in line with God's word? Why do I always get attack spiritually? Are my actions or thinking opening the door to Satan and his demons? Where does God fit in my schedule? What kind of relationship do I have with the Most High? To draw closer to God, you have to know how you will do it and what you will need to do it. As you test yourself, be realistic. If you set a goal to draw closer to God by praying four times a day, make sure you are committed to doing it. If you do not stay committed, you will get discouraged and think it is too hard, so understand what you can do. Be clear and specific about your goals to draw closer to God. Enlist the help of your friends and family members; make sure they support your decision.

Q&A

These are the most common questions asked by new believers or people trying to draw closer to God. My answers are not set in stone, you have to decide what is right for your life after the Most High has provided you confirmation. My answers and suggestions are based on my personal experiences and what I have learned to draw closer to God

What is the best bible version to buy or use?

I like a few versions, but I mainly stick with the KJV (King James Version) and NKJV (New King James Version). My personal bible has the Hebrew names of God, such as Yahweh, Elohim, and the Messiah, Yahshua in it. However, I like to look up scriptures in different versions such as the AMP (Amplified bible), and the MSG (The Message). I think the best version will be the one you can understand at the time but one that is not changing the context of the scriptures because many of the "new age" bibles does just that, so be careful. I would suggest no matter what version you are comfortable with, to keep a KJV or NKJV with you. I use and would suggest getting copies of the lost books of the bible, the Apocrypha, a Strong's concordance that contains the Greek and Hebrew explanation, and a bible that has both the Greek and Hebrew definition of words for a more in-depth bible study; the Matthew Henry Commentary for a deeper reading. However, before you get into deeper, readings make sure you understand the bible, as many finds parts contradicting and adding additional readings can add to that, so be careful about how you are interpreting these readings spiritually. Pray before you read, and study and let the Holy Spirit guide you.

How do I study the bible?

Although many read the bible, they do not take the time to study it. The bible is full of spiritual and historical events that cannot be ignored. There are many events that take place in the bible you really need to understand the context, such as why was it stated the way it was, who was it stated to, who wrote it and why, what location does these events take place and what makes it significant, these are some things you will be curious about. Therefore, take the time to study, look up words you don't understand, get some historical background on the locations and the authors. In addition, many names in the bible have a significant meaning, such as when Jacob's name was change to Israel (Yisrael, in Hebrew) in *Genesis 32:28*. The most important part of studying and inquiring about what is going on in the scriptures is to allow the Holy Spirit to reveal the meanings. Many people rely on their pastors to "teach them the bible" but they can only show you so much and they can never show you more than God can, so rely more on what the Holy Spirit is teaching you more than anything. I think the Holy

Spirit is the best Teacher if you ask me! When you take the time to study the bible, you will clearly recognize when people are misusing, twisting scriptures either by error or for their own gain.

When you are going into "study mode," gather all the materials you will use, notebooks, pens, highlighters, sticky notes, dictionaries, etc. Find somewhere that is not distracting and you can start either with a particular scripture or with an entire chapter. As you read the chapter, just read it for the first time like you would read a book then read it a second time making and taking notes. If God is revealing something to you at the moment, don't wait! Write it down immediately. You can write in your notebook, who wrote that chapter, who was it written to, what is the chapter about, summarized the chapter, noting what the message is. What have you found that can be applied to your own life? How did someone handle adversity, enemies, setbacks, etc.? You can come up with your own questions and take the time to do the research. There is no rush to read the bible in a year, in a month, or a week, a day, in a few hours, take your time, it will be worth it! *2 Timothy 2:15.*

I have prayed but nothing seems to work?

Do not get stress about what you think is not working. Everything is in God's timing and trust that God is working behind the scenes. Some prayers take longer than others to manifest.

When you feel you have done all you can through prayer and your actions that is a sign that God is in complete control and now you have to simply wait on him. God won't let anything manifest before it's time no matter how much we pray about it, fast about it, cry about, rolled on the floor over it. He is not moved by our emotions and pity party but moved only by what he feels is the right time. It could be he is testing your patience, is what you want more important than what he wants? Patience is a virtue and you will need a lot with God! He does not move on our timetable but he does and will move. I remember a time where I prayed and fasted over a particular thing and did not get it! After I got over myself, just a few months later God gave me something better. Therefore, God timing is the best and sometimes we won't get what we want, and we have to be humble about it and trust He is the author and finisher of our faith, *Hebrews 12:2*.

Which Church should I attend, there are so many choices?

Finding a church can be a challenge, but do not let that stop you from drawing closer to God. Do not beat yourself up if you do not go to church or have not found a church, God will not disappear and you can still connect with him no matter where you are. You can also connect with like-minded individuals in a group. The ideal church will be one that is rightly dividing the word of God (the bible), one that is not taking scriptures out of context, especially to benefit their own agenda or vision. I suggest of getting a hold of the pastor sermons of the church you want to attend and carefully listen; follow what they are saying and examine the scriptures they are using and how they are using them. Many churches are good at giving you a "show" but what exactly are they teaching you? Sometimes you have to learn to eat the meat and throw out the bone, meaning, you may not find the perfect church, and you may have to pull what is good and throw out what is bad.

Now that I learned how to draw closer to God, will my life be perfect?

I wish I can guarantee you perfection, but that is not reality. You might go through more challenges than ever before when you draw closer to God. Unexpected things will happen. You will be sad, discourage, upset but it will not last, God will restore your joy, *Psalm 30:5*. One family member told me before accepting God, her life was good and fun and now all Hell breaks loose! And that is pretty much what will happen before it gets better. There will be challenges you never experienced as a sinner you will experience as a believer. The devil is no joke; he will be an attack mode constantly. That is why you must become your own prayer warrior and learn to fight back. The devil takes no break, you take no break, stay in prayer. The goal to drawing closer to God is not to have a "perfect life." It is more about humbling yourself to receive the one, and only true God (Yahweh) will for our lives, acknowledging that God is greater than we are and we need him. It is more a heart and spiritual change rather than a change of your surroundings. I encourage you to not be looking to be "perfect" because you'll find you have created your own headache. Instead, submit to God's will and let him lead your life and your life will be perfect in him and to him. *"God is not slow in keeping his promise, as some understand slowness. Instead, he is patient with you, not wanting anyone to perish, but everyone to come to repentance,"* 2 Peter 3:9.

I am married to someone who is not a believer, what should I do?

Live your life according to the scriptures and they may follow, *1 Corinthians 7:12-16*. Most people with common sense who see someone changing for the better will inquire about what is going on and will desire the same. If you are in a marriage like this, be patient. Any relationship where you force things on the person will eventually reach their breaking point and someone will lose the battle. If you are a believer and your spouse is not, you are better off praying to God, so God can step in and you keep out! Sometimes you think your spouse is not listening or paying attention but they are. I know someone whose husband never went to church but when I had a conversation with him, and the bible came up, he knew more about the scriptures than his wife who grew up in church did. Do not be quick to judge, most people know God- they have a different way of showing they know God. In addition, going to church does not make you a believer; it is just something you do as part of your belief. There are plenty of people sitting in church because it has become routine and are completely disconnected with what is going on. The amount of years you have been saved or been going to church means nothing if you still can't or don't apply the scriptures to your life to make changes. Likewise, just because you don't "see" a person go to church doesn't mean they are not studying their bible. In fact, I had a neighbor tell me one time, why don't I go to church on Sunday, after I laughed, I explained to him I observe the Sabbath and I asked him why is he monitoring me, anyway! Creepy! It's not about what you "see" people doing, even God is not concern with appearance, *1 Samuel 16:7; Matthew 23:25-28*; it's about what they are doing privately, especially when no one is looking. Plenty of people go to church and still live a wicked life, church attendance doesn't change everybody. We have to get out of the mentality that because "we" don't "see" others do something like "we" do that they are not doing anything at all. It's not our job to be monitoring people lives. The most important thing you can do is monitor your own life, live accordingly to God's will, and the person you're trying to see the "light" might just want to know about God themselves.

How can I get my family members, and friends to believe?

I am a big proponent on not forcing people into doing anything they do not want to do. Forcing beliefs on people will make them not believe and they will draw away from you. God gave us free will and we should allow people, even family members to ultimately decide, *Mark 8:34-38; Revelation 3:20; Ezekiel*

18:30-32; John 1:12-13; Deuteronomy 30:19-20; 2 Timothy 2:26; John 3:16; Psalm 37:23; John 6:44. Your behavior as a believer is a better testimony than your words to others. Even if you convince the person to believe they still have to confess Yahshua on their own and make a life change on their own. Scripture says "work out your own salvation with fear and trembling," *Philippians 2:12-13.* You can't force open their mouth or heart to make the confession *"that if you confess with your mouth the Messiah Yahshua, and believe in your heart that God has raised him from the dead, you shall be saved. For with the heart one believes unto righteousness, and with them mouth confession is made unto salvation," Romans 10:9-10.* Do you want to put your family member in a position of believing just because you want them to believe or would you prefer they make a heartfelt submission to God? We should share, encourage, and teach others about God but we cannot force them. If someone is adamant about not hearing anything about God leave them alone, *Matthew 10:14.* Now this applies to the ones who don't want to hear it, but if someone wants to learn by all means share, teach them.

I do wholeheartedly believe you should still raise your children to know God, obey, and encourage them to have a relationship with him. God made that clear in several scriptures, *Deuteronomy 11:18-19; Deuteronomy 6:4-7; Proverbs 22:6* but even your children have to ultimately make a final decision, especially for those receiving the information at a young age. For those who became a believer later in life and your children are adults now, the best way to make believers out of non-believers is how you live your life. If people see God has been good to you, they will want some God in their life. If they see God has changed your attitude and behavior into something good, they will want to know who your God is, *Ruth 1:6-19*. In any case, don't worry, God often make the ultimate decision, *Proverbs 16:9 (NIV)* **"In their hearts humans plan their course, but God establishes their steps."**

I have tried to be good and live holy, but it is just not working for me, what am I doing wrong?

Before you get down on yourself, I want to encourage you and let you know you are not alone, many people have something they are dealing with and feel they cannot stop. The best way to conform to living holy is to renew your mind on what God says in the bible. If you are not reading your bible, studying it, and living it out in your life, you will always slip up. Decide with your heart and mind, is what I am doing more important than what God wants me to do? Is that thing in my life keeping me from being holy more than God? God himself says he is holy therefore, you be holy, *Leviticus 20:26, 1 Peter 1:16*, God wants us to be like him. He wants us to be separated and sanctified from sin and the likeness. Everything you do with God and for God will involve a heart change. Whatever is keeping you from being holy holds a special place in your heart and you will need to address it, pray for it to be removed and let God burn that desire that keeps it alive in your heart then take actions against it. For instance, let us say you struggle with fornication. Fornication is a sin of the flesh, to conquer fornication, you look up scriptures such as, *1 Corinthians 6:18-20; 1 Corinthians 10:13; 1 Thessalonians 4:3-4; Colossians 3:5; 2 Timothy 2:22*, and meditate on them daily, pray, then take actions to not fornicate. For instance, don't cater to things that ignite the desire to fornicate, such as watching porn, videos, and pictures of people showing their body parts, partying. If you are dating, make it clear what you will not do. The person who truly cares about you will understand. However, you need to be the decision maker concerning your holiness. You can't get in the mental state thinking you have no control of your behavior. If you don't have a disability and you are not mentally challenged, you can control the choices you make. We have a part to play as well in our quest to holiness. You can submit to your flesh or submit to God's spirit, *1 Corinthians 6:12-20*.

Why do people assume you are judging them when you try to correct them concerning the things of God?

Many people often get upset when people correct them and feel they are being "judge." I love the scripture *Proverbs 9:8-10* and it says, *"Reprove not a scorner, lest he hate thee; rebuke a wise man, and he will love three." "Give instruction to a wise man, and he will be yet wiser: teach a just man, and he will increase in learning." "The fear of Yahweh is the beginning of wisdom, and the knowledge of the Holy One is understanding."* Not everyone is wise and can take correction; some people are comfortable in their foolishness, *Proverbs 1:7*, the wise, will not take it as judgment. I also love *Galatians 4:16 "Am I therefore become your enemy, because I tell you the truth?"* Some people really can't handle the truth. They don't want to hear it. Often people will tell you the bible say not to judge, *Matthew 7:1-3*, which is correct, but that is for those making hypocritical judgments or criticizing based on opinions. However, since most people like to pick scriptures fitting for them they neglect *John 7:24* where is says, *"Judge not according to the appearance, but judge righteous judgment."* Righteousness judgment is judging according to God's word. You will find in the bible where God would instruct others to judge the people, *1 Corinthians 5:9-13; 1 Corinthians 6:1-5*; the book of Judges is based on God raising Judges to "judge" the people out of sin and for rebelling against him according to God's word. Believers can judge other believers based on God's word, but it is done to guide the person out of sin not for being mean. For instance, if your sister or brother in the church (*the church is a body of people, not the building*) is stuck in a sin, you can remind them what the scriptures say about that sin. Now, don't get crazy here, I wouldn't go around tapping people on the head with the bible just to make a point. Righteous judgment should be fair and done out of love to see someone repent and turn back to God. We should not be harsh with our words and coming down on others like a gavel. Remember, *"Pleasant words are like honeycomb, sweet and delightful to the soul and healing to the body," Proverbs 16:24*.

Why does God allow bad things to happen, especially to good people or innocent people?

That is one of the most challenging questions to be asked as a believer of God. There is no true answer because God is the "I AM" He makes the ultimate decision, *Exodus 3:14; John 8:58; Revelation 1:8.* Only God knows the spiritual implications of his actions. We can try to come up with some reasons, but none would truly answer this question. It may just be something we all wait until we get to Heaven to ask ourselves. We must trust that God knows what he is doing and why he is doing it. Many times non-believers will challenge you with questions like this, so they can have a reason not to believe God exists, but trying to figure God out logically or scientifically will never work because God is a spirit. Knowing this allows me to understand that God sees more than we can comprehend in the spiritual world. The best thing to do when you see bad things happening to good people, or to you, is trust God is in control, pray that he gives you spiritual understanding and revelation concerning the matter and never stop believing God loves you.

TAKING STEPS TO DRAW CLOSER TO GOD

• CONCLUSION •

Drawing closer to God is a process, and it will not happen overnight. When you draw closer to God, you are deciding to change your heart, mind, and actions to do the will of God for your life. You are deciding to please him and not yourself. You are also building a relationship with him. If you have turned away from God and now want to draw closer to him, use these five steps. In your quest, also examine yourself. What drew you away from God or what drew you to him? What did you make priority over God over the years? Who and what distracted you from God? Reflect on your answers and examine yourself. Your bible will be your treasure and the most important tool in achieving your goal of drawing closer to God.

When you take the time to read your bible and meditate on scriptures, it will shape you and transform. Will you take the initiative? Can he be the priority in your life? Is he worth it to you? If you answered yes to all of these questions, then I encourage you to start by taking these steps to drawing closer to him. First, seek him; second, trust him; third, make a commitment to him; forth, pray; fifth, love and last, pass the test and your desire to draw close to him will be fulfilled. I want to encourage you to take these steps sincerely. I have taken these steps myself and can tell you that you are guaranteed to be blessed by God in every way when you seek him. My spiritual life over the years has increased. I feel so love and protected by God because of the relationship I have with him. God is waiting and wants to draw closer to you, *James 4:8, Jeremiah 24:7.*

TAKING STEPS TO DRAW CLOSER TO GOD

• SALVATION •

I wrote this book with the assumption you are already a born-again believer. However, if you are not born-again, salvation is available to you. Here is an understanding of what salvation is about, *When you decide to accept Yahshua as Savior, you are accepting he died on the cross and shed his blood for your sins. You are deciding and stating to God that your life is his. You are deciding to enter his kingdom and be his child.* Salvation involves a few steps, and I will share with you what these steps are:

First, you admit that you are a sinner. We are all born into sin; it is not about what you did, **Psalm 51:5.**

Second, you need to repent of your sins, **1 John 1:9.** Repentance is a self-acknowledgement of your sins and your commitment to God about changing. It's' a heartfelt, sincere apology and your commitment to change for the better based on God's word through your actions. It is turning away from your sins to God and his righteousness.

Third, you must believe and confess that Yahshua died for your sins, and believe in your heart that God raised him from the dead, **John 3:16, Romans 5:8, Romans 10:9-10.**

After reading and meditating on the scriptures given, do you understand salvation? The decision is yours to make. Nobody can force you. It is your decision and if you already decided that salvation is for you then pray this prayer out loud and believe it in your heart as you pray:

Father, In the name of Yahshua, I repent of all my sins. I confess with my mouth Yahshua as my Savior and believe in my heart he died on the cross for my sins and Yahweh rose him up after three days. I invite Yahshua to sit, rule and reign on the throne of my life. I believe I receive my salvation right now. Amen.

If this was your first time saying the salvation prayer, I want to congratulate you on the decision you made to accept Yahshua as your Savior! I encourage you to read, study your bible, pray, fellowship with God and other believers, and apply these steps to your life. As you do this your life will change, and you will draw closer to God.

Please note, saying this prayer is not the end of it all, the most important thing you can do after believing and confessing is being obedient to God. You may also not feel an "immediate" change. Now it's time for you to get serious about establishing a relationship with God by drawing closer to him, so you can start to see a change. The bible says for us to work out our own salvation, *Philippians 2:12-13*, so you have work to do!

TAKING STEPS TO DRAW CLOSER TO GOD

"For He satisfies the longing soul and fills the hungry soul with goodness" ~ Psalm 107:9

ABOUT THE AUTHOR

Milly J was born and raised in New York. With an interest in writing since childhood, Milly J has always concentrated her writing on fiction. It was not until she became a born-again believer she developed a passion for writing about spiritual things and seeing others spiritually grow. Her educational background includes a B.A. in Criminal Justice from John Jay College, and M.A. in Forensic Psychology. Milly J enjoys reading, writing, traveling, and watching cooking shows.

Connect with Milly J
Website: www.TheMillyJ.com